WE BELIEVE Series

BASICS OF CHRISTIANITY

JESUS

Knowing Our Savior

MAX ANDERS

THOMAS NELSON PUBLISHERS

Nashville • Atlanta • London • Vancouver

Published in Nashville, Tennessee, by Thomas Nelson, Inc.

Unless otherwise indicated, Scripture quotations are from the *New King James Version of the Bible,* © 1979, 1980, 1982, Thomas Nelson, Inc., Publishers.

Scripture quotations identified by NASB are from the *New American Standard Bible,* © The Lockman Foundation 1960, 1962, 1963, 1968, 1971, 1973, 1975, 1977, and used by permission.

Library of Congress Cataloging-in-Publication Information

Anders, Max E., 1947–
    Jesus : knowing our Saviour / Max Anders.
    (We believe series)
    Includes bibliographical references.
    ISBN 0–8407–8486–4
    1. Jesus Christ—Person and offices. 2. Jesus Christ—Teachings.
  3. Jesus Christ—Knowableness. I. Title. II. Series: We believe series
(Thomas Nelson Publishers)
BT207.A53   1995   94–45930
232'.07—dc20   CIP

Printed in the United States of America

1 2 3 4 5 6 7 8—00 99 98 97 96 95

Contents

Introduction to the We Believe! Basics of Christianity Series

In his book, *Mere Christianity*, C.S. Lewis, a well-known Christian writer from Great Britain, wrote:

> Everyone has warned me not to tell you what I am going to tell you . . . They all say "the ordinary reader does not want Theology; give him plain practical religion." I have rejected their advice. I do not think the ordinary reader is such a fool. Theology means "the science of God," and I think any man who wants to think about God at all would like to have the clearest and most accurate ideas about Him which are available. You are not children: why should you be treated like children?
>
> Theology is practical. Everyone reads, everyone hears things discussed. Consequently if you do not listen to Theology, that will not mean that you have no ideas about God. It will mean that you have a lot of wrong ones—bad, muddled, out-of-date ideas. For a great many of the ideas about God which are trotted out as novelties today, are simply the ones which real Theologians tried centuries ago and rejected. To believe in the popular religion of modern England (or America) is retrogression—like believing the earth is flat (135–136).

We want to be sure, as we navigate the sea of life, that we are not thinking we might drop off the edge, or that monsters lurk in the deep, or that the stars determine our destiny. We must think accurately. We must have truth. We must anchor ourselves to reality. Anything else is not only retrogression; it is unfulfilling, self-defeating, and even dangerous.

That is why this series was written. We are in a time of unprecedented upheaval in American culture. For over two centuries, many who lived in the United States believed in God and had a basic understanding of the Bible. But today, after one or two short generations of rapid social change, masses of Americans know nearly nothing about the Bible. When these people come into the church, they are not grounded in the same teachings as those who have grown up in the church. The result is a congregation of people who do not share a common knowledge base. And any group that lacks such a base cannot experience complete unity, and it cannot easily move in one direction as a congregation.

The lack of knowledge common to all members hampers a church's effectiveness in three other cases: First, when new people come into the church thinking they know the truth about God, Jesus, and the Bible, but they don't. They picked up inaccurate information before coming into the church. Now they can be divisive, perhaps innocently, and can lead others into error.

Second is the case when Christians know quite a bit about one subject, but very little about another. For example, they may be interested in prophecy but know almost nothing about the deity of Christ. These are vulnerable to error about Jesus Himself, and despite their enthusiasm for prophecy (or it could be any other doctrine), their personal life is weakened, as well as the life of their church.

Third, churches today often are made up of people with several to many different church backgrounds. In the diversity of experiences lies precious strength, but only as that diversity arises from a common core of belief about Christian essentials.

If any church is to be successful, the core of the congregation must together build upon a common base of accurate knowledge that corresponds to the one who is Truth. I hope that this series of books will help churches all across America (and even around the world) provide this crucial base of knowledge and thus be more securely attached to the church's Head, Jesus Christ.

One final word about how to use the book. It is structured so that an individual can go through it on his or her own or so that it can be used by a small group or Sunday school class. Please note the end-of-chapter reviews (Speed Bump!), self-tests (Fill In the Blank), discussion questions, guided further study, and so on. Whether you are using the book alone or with a group, I hope that you will use this material to help you get the most out of the book.

How To Teach this Book

The books in this series are written so that they can be used as a thirteen-week curriculum, ideal for Sunday school classes or other small-group meetings. You will notice that there only twelve chapters—to allow for a session when you may want to do something else. Every quarter seems to call for at least one different type of session, because of holidays, summer vacation, or other special events. If you use all twelve chapters, and still have a session left in the quarter, have a fellowship meeting with refreshment, and use the time to get to know others better. Or use the session to invite newcomers in hopes they will continue with the course.

All ten books in the series together form a "Basic Knowledge Curriculum" for Christians. Certainly Christians would eventually want to know more than is in these books, but they should not know less. Therefore, the series is excellent for seekers, for new Christians, and for Christians who may not have a solid foundation of biblical education. It is also a good series for those whose biblical education has been spotty.

Of course, the books can also be used in small groups and discipleship groups. If you are studying the book by yourself, you can simply read the chapters and go through the material at the end. If you are using the books to teach outhers, you might find the following guidelines helpful·

(handwritten: ① Prayer ⑥ closing prayer ② Quiz ③ summarize material ④ discuss chapter ⑤ question/answer)

Teaching Outline

1. Begin the session with prayer.

2. Consider having a quiz at the beginning of each meeting over the self-test from the chapter to be studied for that day. The quiz can be optional, or the group may want everyone to commit to it, depending on the setting in which the material is taught. In a small discipleship group or one-on-one, it might be required. In a larger Sunday school class, it might need to be optional.

3. At the beginning of the session, summarize the material. You may want to have class members be prepared to summarize the material. You might want to bring in information that was not covered in the book. There might be some in the class who have not read the material, and this will help catch them up with those who did. Even for those who did read it, a summary will refresh their minds and get

everyone into a common mind-set. It may also generate questions and discussion.

4. Discuss the material at the end of the chapters as time permits. Use whatever you think best fits the group.

5. Have a special time for questions and answers, or encourage questions during the course of discussion. If you are asked a question you can't answer (it happens to all of us), just say you don't know, but that you will find out, Then, the following week, you can open the question and answer time, or perhaps the discussion time, with the answer to the question from last week.

6. Close with prayer.

You may have other things you would like to incorporate, and flexibility is the key to success. These suggestions are given only to guide, not to dictate. Prayerfully, choose a plan suited to your circumstances.

*The nature of Christ's existence is
mysterious, I admit; but this mystery meets
the wants of man—reject it and the world is
an inexplicable riddle; believe it, and the
history of our race is satisfactorily explained.*
■ **Napoleon**

1

Who Is Jesus?

I'm a sucker for good rescue stories. To me, they are exciting, rewarding, and heartwarming. There is something special about hearing of someone who is lost, without hope, and rescued just in time by the heroic efforts of another. Each time I read a rescue story, I am deeply moved by the selflessness of people who risk their own safety to rescue others whom they may never have met.

One of the most amazing rescue stories I know about occurred in July of 1976 when, in a swift display of military precision, courage, and sheer daring, Israeli commandos rescued 102 Jewish hostages from Uganda, in Central East Africa. Their plane had been hijacked by Palestinian terrorists and flown to that safe haven protected by the monstrous madman, dictator Idi Amin. The hostages were probably good as dead if something could not be done to save them. Something was done.

The dramatic series of events began shortly after noon, Sunday, June 27, when a white Air France Airbus lifted off the runway at the Athens International Airport. It banked west, then began the flight over the brilliant blue gulf of Corinth and on to the Aegean Sea. It was a beautiful day to fly, a sharp contrast to the events to follow.

The serenity of the early moments of the flight was shattered by a scream as a man and a woman jumped to their feet, brandishing hand grenades, quickly training pistols on the flight attendants. The man stepped toward the pilot's cabin and ordered the plane taken to the airport at Entebbe, the capital of Uganda. The goal—to force Israel and four other nations to release fifty–three Palestinian or pro-Palestinian terrorists from jail. They made it clear that if the jailed terrorists were not freed, the 102 hostages would be slaughtered like diseased cattle.

Two days later, two thousand miles away, the leaders of Israel sat in the wood-paneled Cabinet Room of the Israeli Knesset. Weary and anxious, they had to face still another threat to their people. In addition to the safety of the Jewish people aboard the flight, they had to consider another issue: If the terrorists got away with this, more acts of violence and terrorism would follow. No Israeli would be safe unless the terrorists could be stopped.

Yitzhak Rabin, the prime minister, Lt. Gen. Mordechai Gur, the military chief of staff, and all the cabinet members decided they should explore the possibility of negotiating a release without bloodshed. But at the same time, they would make an all-out effort to come up with a military option. They had no reason to believe the terrorists would negotiate honorably.

Immediately, a strike force was assembled on a military base in the Israeli desert to begin planning the impossible: a raid on Entebbe to save the hostages. Staff members of El Al, the Israeli national airlines, gave information about possible flight routes, refueling opportunities, and communication facilities. Israel slipped secret agents into Uganda to analyze the situation. Information began pouring back.

On June 30 and July 1, the terrorists released all non-Jewish passengers. This was good news, because fewer hostages increased the chances of success. Israeli intelligence learned that the hostages were being kept in the central open area of the small airport terminal building in the capital city, and that the airport was not wired with explosives. It was another good sign that the terrorists and the Ugandans hadn't considered the possibility of a rescue attempt. The United States gave Israel satellite photographs of the airport, and Kenya gave secret assurances that an Israeli strike force would be allowed to land at Nairobi to refuel and, on the return trip, care for any wounded.

The raiding party was selected and honed to a strike force specially trained in air-assault operations. They were among the finest military men in the world, led by thirty-year-old Col. Jonathan Netanyahu, who had moved to Israel from the United States when he was only two. Deep in the desert at the isolated military base, they practiced the raid again and again, shaving the ground rescue time down to fifty-five minutes.

The airplanes chosen to take the strike team to Entebbe were four U.S.-built Hercules C-130 cargo planes and two Boeing 707 jets. One jet was an airborne command-and-communications center and the other was a hospital plane. The six planes followed El Al's usual route to South Africa: down the Red Sea and over Ethiopia and Kenya. The hospital plane landed in Nairobi. The five military aircraft left the

Nairobi landing pattern and redirected toward Entebbe. No suspicion was aroused anywhere, because it was assumed that the radar reading of the planes, to this point, was the normal El Al flight to South Africa. The planes then dropped very low to escape radar and flew directly to the airport at Entebbe.

As one cargo plane rolled to a stop in the darkness—as yet undetected because the airport was not being used—its huge tail ramp dropped and out came a large, black Mercedes Benz limousine, closely followed by two Land Rovers filled with Israeli commandos dressed in Palestinian uniforms. In the back of the limousine was a bulky Israeli officer dressed like dictator Idi Amin. The license plate on the limousine was identical to that of Amin's official car. As the party drove up to the terminal building, the Ugandan guards snapped to attention, allowing the Israeli commandos to get within a few yards of the building before the first shots were fired.

Bullets were soon raining on the airport like hail in a thunderstorm. Within ten to twenty minutes, the shooting was over. The commandos ordered the hostages to the planes that were waiting in takeoff position, engines still running. As the hostages ran to the planes, great fireballs erupted in the distance as Israeli commandos blew up the eleven parked MiG jets that would have scrambled to intercept the escaping Israeli planes. As the hostages and commandos rushed onto the huge Hercules, the rear hatch slammed shut. Fifty-three minutes after the raid began, the planes began moving into position for takeoff. The hostages were saved!

What will move one person to risk death in order that another might live?

The rescue was not letter perfect. Three hostages lost their lives. That was deeply saddening, but all of them may have died otherwise. Remarkably, only one Israeli commando lost his life—the assault-force commander, Col. Jonathan Netanyahu. A sniper in the control tower killed him with a bullet in the back. Netanyahu gave his life to save others.

Stories like this cause me to ask what will move one person to risk death in order that another person might live? Why would Col. Netanyahu risk his life to save someone else from death? If someone is going to die, isn't it "better him than me?"

To me, this willingness to risk on behalf of others is part of the image of God in man. Something placed by God deep in the core of our being allows us to put ourselves in the helpless person's shoes, imagine what a terror they are experiencing, and say, "If I were him, I

would long for someone to rescue me; therefore, I'll try to rescue him."
God's image within us gives rise to this nobility, this courage, dignity,
and honor.

As great as the mission at Entebbe was, it pales in comparison to
the greatest rescue in history—the saving of mankind by God.
Mankind found itself lost in life, held hostage by evil, helpless and
hopeless. Jesus risked Himself—even gave His life—to rescue
mankind. His is the greatest of all acts, marked with nobility, dignity,
and honor. "Rescue" resides within the heart of God.

In this chapter we learn that . . .

1. Jesus of Nazareth is the divine Son of God, the second member of the
   Trinity and the Savior of humanity.
2. the Scriptures declare Him to be God, and His words and works prove
   Him to be God.
3. the Scriptures declare Him to be a man, and His words and works prove
   Him to be a man.

Jesus is the Great Rescuer. He is the one figure in history who
stands above all others. His life is the greatest ever lived. But who is
this Jesus? Who is this modest man from Galilee who turned the world
on its ear in three short years of itinerant preaching? Who is this one
who is still alive and for whom many people would willingly die?
How can we explain His impact on the world? The answers to these
questions form the basis of our look at Jesus of Nazareth in this book.

Allow me to tell you the story of my encounter with Him. My
mother took me to church from my earliest days, teaching me that
there was a God. There was never a day when I did not believe in God
and that Jesus was the Son of God. I went to church virtually every
Sunday until I was tall enough to look my mother in the eye. Then, because my father and two older brothers did not go to church, I refused
to go, but I never stopped believing.

I was not a Christian at that time. Although I believed, I had never
made a personal commitment to follow Jesus. I became a Christian a
number of years later. It happened in my first year in college during a
time of personal crisis. I was struggling to find something worth living for. In the absence of something to stand for, I was falling for anything. Once, during a great flood of guilt for my personal sins and
deep distress over the meaninglessness of my life, I began sinking in
despair. I grabbed the first thing I thought would keep me afloat, and
that was Jesus. A friend presented the gospel of Christ to me, and I

committed my life to Him, and found great relief from the emotional pain of this world as well as hope for the next.

Some years later, I found myself in another personal crisis. I became exceedingly troubled over the doctrine of hell. I could not reconcile my belief in a God of grace with a God who could create a place like hell. If I were God, I reasoned, I would be willing to forego creating the world as we know it if I knew that even one person would go to hell as a result of my creation.

That got me to thinking. Maybe Christianity *wasn't* the only true or valid religion. I embarked on a resolute attempt to "un-believe." I wanted another option. I had not given Christianity a lot of scrutiny before I became a Christian. I just grabbed it because it was the only thing I saw to grasp in my moment of deep distress. If I had grown up a Muslim and fallen away, I probably would have reverted back to Islam, not to Christianity, I reasoned. The same would have been true if I had grown up a Jew. Maybe I was a Christian, I told myself, not because Christianity was true but simply because my mother took me to church when I was young, and it was the only option I knew of.

That did not seem like an adequate reason for me to stake my life on Christianity. So, I began to try to convert *from* Christianity. I began looking at all the other religions. I learned of the Koran, the writings of Islam. I read Hindu writings. I read books on comparative religions. But, none of them satisfied. They all seemed like inferior imitations of divine writings.

"Rescue" resides within the heart of God.

Then one day, I was reading in chapter 6 of the Gospel of John. This passage tells about Jesus teaching the multitudes a very difficult teaching. He said, "Unless you eat the flesh of the Son of Man and drink His blood, you have no life in yourselves" (verse 53 NASB).

He was using a figure of speech, meaning that unless they took unto themselves the Son of Man—unless they believed in Him and embraced Him—they did not have eternal life. But the multitude was not listening with a "spiritual" ear, and they thought He was talking cannibalism. They turned on their heels and left in disgust.

Jesus then turned to His disciples and said, "Do you also want to go away?" (verse 67). Simon Peter answered Him, "Lord, to whom shall we go? You have the words of eternal life" (verse 68).

Something deep within me responded to that passage of scripture. Something that was withered and dry stirred with new life at those words. *Here I have been looking around at every other religion to find a substitute for Christ, I thought, and I have not been able to find one. For every problem that I solve by giving up Christ, I create a hundred in its place.* I wanted a religion that had no problems, where every puzzle was solved. I found this was not possible. No religion is without puzzles. Nor is atheism. So, I decided I would not be able to have a world view without problems; but I determined to choose the one that I thought had the fewest problems. Easily, that was Christianity. <u>True Christianity is simply Jesus Christ and a personal relationship with Him.</u> *Yes !*

Lord, I still don't understand why you created hell, I thought. But there are no answers outside of you. If I want something else, to whom shall I go? You have the words of eternal life.

Yes, there are hard things about Jesus and His teachings, just as the multitude in John 6 found Jesus' teachings difficult. The hardness, I believe, however, comes not from His teaching but from our own limitations. Notice that Peter did not say He understood all of Jesus' teachings. He affirmed that he had heard enough to know that, even when he came up against something that was hard to understand, he would not let that destroy what he did understand. When I reasoned through all that, in the proverbial "twinkling of an eye," I was once again secure in Christ, and I have never wavered since. Jesus, I believe, is the answer to whatever the question is about life and after-life.

What Do You Mean When You Say "Jesus"?

Jesus of Nazareth is the divine Son of God, the second member of the Trinity and the Savior of humanity.

If you were to ask ten people at random who Jesus is, you would probably get ten different answers. To some, He is merely a man, like any other human being. To others, he is a great moral teacher, the founder of one of the world's great religions. To others, he is a madman, instigator of much of the evil in the world (consider the Crusades, the Spanish Inquisition, the religious wars, the "colonialistic evangelism and corruption" of Third-World cultures). Others have no idea who He is, and still others believe He never existed. To many, He is nothing but a name to curse and swear by. Therefore, as the starting point for our study of Him, we must agree on who and what we mean when we say "Jesus."

When I say "Jesus," I mean that He is the Son of God, the second member of the Trinity who existed before the creation of the world, who participated with the Father and the Holy Spirit in creation, and who became human. This Jesus of Nazareth, being born of a virgin, came to earth to do the will of God the Father. He died for our sins, came to life again, was bodily resurrected, ascended into heaven, and will come again some day to judge sin and establish permanent righteousness on earth.

Why Believe Jesus Was God?

We believe Jesus was God because the Scriptures declare Him to be God, and His words and works prove Him to be God.

Having said that, let us look more closely at the specifics. My loose definition has two dimensions: First, Jesus was God, and second, Jesus was man. The Bible teaches this clearly—that He was fully God, and that He was fully man. We read in Philippians 2:6–8:

He existed in the form of God, [but] did not regard equality with God a thing to be grasped, but emptied Himself, taking the form of a bond-servant, and being made in the likeness of men. And being found in appearance as a man, He humbled Himself by becoming obedient to the point of death, even death on a cross (NASB).

There it is in black and white. He was God and He was man.

Second Member of the Trinity

As God, Jesus is the second member of the Trinity. We deal more fully with the Trinity in the book in this series titled *God: Knowing Our Creator.* Suffice it to say that, in historical Christian teaching, the doctrine of the Trinity states that God is one being, and yet three "persons." Although the terminology is difficult to understand, theologians and Bible teachers say God was "one God in substance but three in subsistence." It is impossible for our finite minds to comprehend this teaching fully, and yet the Bible teaches it. God is one and yet three (within the one).

This statement is an "antinomy," which means "two apparently mutually exclusive truths which must be embraced simultaneously." The truths are not really mutually exclusive, or else God would be the author of nonsense, which He isn't. But with our limited information and intellectual capacity, the statements about God being one, yet three *appears to be* mutually exclusive.

With that assumption, God the Father, God the Son, and God the Holy Spirit are the three members of the Trinity.

Jesus, then, is God, or the second member of the Trinity. If that is the case, Jesus existed before He was born as Jesus of Nazareth. God has no beginning and no end. Jesus is God. Therefore, Jesus has no beginning and no end. This is supported in John 8:58. When Jesus was talking to some hostile religious leaders, He said, "Before Abraham (the ancient ancestor of all Jews) was born, I AM." This was a claim by Jesus that He existed before Abraham was born two thousand years before Jesus came to earth. In addition, His words "I AM" are a reference to the sacred name of God, Jehovah, and therefore, a claim to be God. Jesus also claimed to exist before the world began (John 17:5).

Jesus' Old Testament Names

If Jesus existed before he was born as Jesus of Nazareth, what was His name, and what did He do? We don't know for sure, but we can gather some facts from pertinent information. We meet Jesus in the Old Testament as the "Captain of the Hosts of the Lord." In the book of Joshua, for example, Joshua was studying how to conquer the city of Jericho. Suddenly, out of nowhere, a man stood before him. We can imagine that Joshua might have put his hand on his sword. He asked, "Are you friend or are you foe?"

The "man" answered, "I indeed come now as captain of the host of the Lord." The Bible reports that "Joshua fell on his face to the earth, and bowed down, and said to Him, 'What has my lord to say to his servant?' And the captain of the Lord's host said to Joshua, 'Remove your sandals from your feet, for the place where you are standing is holy.' And Joshua did so." (Joshua 5:13–15 NASB) We can assume from this that the "Captain of the Hosts of the Lord" was divine, because angels never accept the worship of men (Revelation 19:10).

In the Old Testament we also encounter someone called "the Angel of the Lord." We assume this was the second member of the Trinity before He took on the bodily form of Jesus of Nazareth. The reason we deduce this is that in Exodus chapter 3 Moses saw a bush that was burning but not consumed. "And the angel of the Lord appeared to him in a blazing fire from the midst of a bush" (verse 2). Then, "when the LORD saw that [Moses] turned aside to look, God called to him from the midst of the bush" (verse 4). The Lord and the Angel of the Lord worked together in this remarkable manifestation to Moses.

And, just as the Captain of the Hosts of the Lord told Joshua to take off his shoes, because the ground he was standing on was holy (because of the presence of the Lord), so the Angel of the Lord told Moses to take off his shoes because the ground was holy. We can assume that the Angel of the Lord and the Captain of the Hosts of the Lord are both divine, but are not God the Father. My educated guess is that this was Jesus before He came to earth as Jesus of Nazareth. It is also interesting that we don't encounter the Captain of the Army of the Lord or the Angel of the Lord in the New Testament after Jesus of Nazareth was born.

Why I need to know who Jesus is:

Today, there is no common understanding of who Jesus is. Many people make up their own definition of who He is. We must be sure we are talking about the same person when we address the question, "Who is Jesus?"

So, while we don't know what name the Son of God had (other than the name LORD) before He appeared as Jesus of Nazareth, we know that he was called the Angel of the Lord, and the Captain of the Hosts of the Lord.

Jesus' Role in Creation

In addition to being involved in certain events of the Old Testament as the Angel of the Lord, Jesus was also involved in the creation of the world. The apostle John states that "all things came into being through Him; and apart from Him nothing came into being" (John 1:3 NASB). The apostle Paul wrote, "For in Him (Jesus) all things were created, both in the heavens and on earth, visible and invisible, whether thrones or dominions or rulers or authorities—all things have been created by Him and for Him" (Colossians 1:16 NASB).

So, in summary, while we don't know what name the second member of the Trinity went by before He became Jesus of Nazareth, we know that He existed before the creation of the world. In fact, as God, He has always existed. Through Him the universe was created, and He was active in the affairs of people in the Old Testament.

Why Believe Jesus Was a Man?

We believe Jesus was a man because the Scriptures declare Him to be a man, and His words and works prove Him to be a man.

Not only was Jesus God; He was also man. His humanity, as we read about it in the Scriptures, is clear. He was born an infant, grew as normal people grow (Luke 2:52), was raised in a normal family environment, got tired (John 4:6), hungry (Matthew 4:2), thirsty (John 19:28), had emotions (Matthew 9:6), and eventually died. We might summarize His humanity by saying, "Jesus was a first-century Jew who lived in Palestine during the reign of Tiberius Caesar. His early life was spent as a carpenter, and later He was an itinerant preacher. He claimed to be the Messiah, the savior of the world, and the deliverer of the Jews. He was executed by crucifixion under Pontius Pilate after a brief life of thirty three years."

Jesus' Impact on History

Jesus has had a profound impact on the history of the world. We now date our calendars and history with the date of His birth. In Western Europe, Great Britain, and the United States, the entire legal system is rooted in His teachings. Slavery was assaulted in the name of Christ, first in England and then in the United States. Schools have been built in the name of Christ. Harvard, Yale, and Princeton were originally schools established to train clergy. Wherever biblical Christianity has taken root in primitive societies, people have stopped killing and eating each other, and they have put on clothes, been educated, and, in modern times, received medical treatment. Certainly, bad things have been done in the name of Christ, but we can't blame Him for those. We must blame faulty and misguided followers of Christ.

In the name of Jesus, Mother Teresa ministers to the sick and dying in India and throughout the world. In His name, multiplied tens of thousands have gone to the mission field to help improve the human condition while carrying the message of salvation. In the name of Jesus, Billy Graham has preached to more people than any other human being alive. In the name of Jesus, Chuck Colson of Watergate infamy exited from his time in prison only to dedicate his life to taking the gospel to prisoners all over the world.

Jesus of Nazareth's Beginnings

Where did this person who has impacted the world so profoundly have his beginnings? Nearly 2,000 years ago in Palestine, a country about 130 miles long and an average of 35 to 40 miles wide. It is a tiny country. There are *counties* in Arizona larger than the entire area of Palestine. Palestine is the ancestral home of the Jews, with Jerusalem being its historical capital. Palestine in the time of Jesus was ruled by Rome. Herod the Great was the Roman governor of that region when Jesus was born.

Herod was cruel, immoral, and not very wise. But he was a great builder, responsible for a magnificent temple which he built for the Jewish population, as well as many other notable structures in and around Jerusalem. He was half Jew himself, so he had an understanding of Jewish values and cultures.

The Roman Emperor during the time when Jesus was born was Augustus, a brilliant politician and military man whose cunning allowed him to rise to power above his competitors. There was an enforced peace in the Mediterranean world at the time, which set the stage for the coming of Jesus. There were no wars within the Roman boundaries, and trade and travel were expedited by the system of Roman roads. There was, perhaps, no better time in history for a universal message to be communicated.

Jesus was born to Mary and Joseph, two faithful Jews who brought Him up in the traditions and orthodoxy of the Jewish faith. His birth was not a normal one, however. God caused a miraculous conception to occur, and Jesus was born of a virgin. Mary and Joseph were living at the time in Nazareth, which is in the northern part of Palestine. An important prophecy in Micah 5:2 declared that the Messiah must be born in Bethlehem, to the south.

After God revealed to Mary and Joseph that the child in Mary's womb would be the Messiah, a decree went out from the Roman emperor Augustus that a census should be taken of the Roman empire. The Romans wanted to improve their system for taxing their subjects, and so they required the registration of names and property. This was the first step in a new levy of taxes.

The Jews had a custom of claiming the home town of their ancestors, depending on which Jewish clan or tribe they were from. Joseph was from the House of David (Israel's greatest king), who was from the city of Bethlehem, a small town just a few miles from the capital, Jerusalem. This meant that Mary and Joseph had to travel from the village they lived in, Nazareth, to Joseph's ancestral village, Bethlehem, to be registered there. In the providence of God, Mary gave birth to Jesus during that trip. Jesus was born in Bethlehem, fulfilling the Messianic prophecy. Mary and Joseph's plan was almost certainly to return to Nazareth as soon as they had fulfilled their responsibility in the census. However, other events intervened, and they did not get back to Nazareth for some time.

Jesus' Cultural Context

The Romans stationed soldiers in Palestine to enforce their occupation of the country. Occupation was like a festering sore to the Jews, who were fiercely independent by nature. On the spiritual side, Jews were not to mix with Gentiles, or non-Jews, in certain affairs, particularly in their religious life. Yet Herod built his own palace beside the Jewish temple, with walls so high that his soldiers could look down into the temple area where only Jews were permitted. This would be like the government of our country placing a video camera in each room of our houses, constantly watching all our activities. To the Jews, Herod's act was a sacrilege and a dehumanizing invasion of privacy.

In the presence of this hated Roman occupation of Palestine, four distinct groups of Jews responded.

The Zealots passionately hated the Romans. They devoted their lives to waging guerrilla warfare against the Romans and regaining their independence.

The Sadducees were prominent Jews with most of the wealth, who were concerned with preserving the comfortable lives they had carved out for themselves. They didn't like the Romans, but they felt that peaceful co-existence with their superiors was the best policy.

The Pharisees were the religious conservatives who held great power over the people. They knew that armed resistance against the Romans was futile, so they tried to carve out a life of tolerance and patience, waiting for the day when the Messiah would come and deliver their nation from the Roman conquerors. The Pharisees developed an elaborate system of laws and customs, and they wove an elaborate tapestry of do's and don'ts around the Old Testament, often violating the Scripture in order to keep their tradition, although they would never admit it.

The religious system of the Pharisees created a sub-culture which helped give the Jews an artificial sense of identity and purpose in the place of their real identity and purpose, which was to live in righteousness as God's people, no matter what the circumstances. Then, they waited and waited, hoping that their faithfulness to the Law would hasten the coming of the Messiah.

The Qumran Community, also known as the Essenes, was a sect which lived in the desert near the Dead Sea in southern Palestine. They were the people who were responsible for preserving the famous Dead Sea Scrolls. They were extremists, who believed that the people of Israel had gone astray, and that they, themselves, were the only true believers. They had a dooms-day mentality, believing that the judgment of God would soon fall upon all the world. So they waited in the desert, in a safe place.

After God's judgment fell, defeating the Romans and chastis-ing the Jews, they would become the leaders of the nation after it was restored to its former greatness. Their community was ap-parently destroyed by the Romans in A.D. 70, under the Emperor Tiberius, who also destroyed the temple in Jerusalem at the same time.

A common thread ran through all four of these groups—a deep and intense longing for the coming of the Messiah. The worse conditions were for the Jews and the less control they had over their destiny, the more they longed for the Messiah to come and deliver them. Some expected a purely political Messiah while others longed for spiritual deliverance and guidance. But among all, the cry was, "O Lord, how long" meaning how long will You wait before you deliver us? Ultimately, this expectation that the Messiah would deliver them from Roman oppression was the major reason for the rejection of Jesus as the Messiah. He offered a spiritual kingdom, which did not satisfy their desire for politi-cal independence.

Into this cultural context Jesus was born. The Bible declares that He was born "in the fullness of time," or at the right time. The heightened expectations and readiness of the Jews along with the political, social, economic, and linguistic establishment of the Roman empire made everything ready. But from the very begin-ning, Jesus did not meet the expectations of the Messianic Hope of the people. Born in a stable, He lived an obscure life as a car-penter in an insignificant Galilean town, and then burst on the scene with a message of redemption which was spiritual, not political.

Jesus the Prophesied Messiah

We mentioned earlier that Jesus had to be born in Bethlehem in order to fulfill the prophecy of the prophet Micah. The journey of Joseph and Mary to this village by the decree of Caesar for the census resulted in that prophecy being fulfilled. This prophecy was not the only one regarding the Messiah which Jesus fulfilled. Josh McDowell, in his excellent book *Evidence That Demands a Verdict*, points out that there are several hundred references to the Messiah in the Old Testament, and that there are sixty-one major prophecies which Jesus clearly fulfilled.

In the New Testament, when the disciples of Jesus appealed to Scripture to demonstrate that Jesus was the Messiah, they appealed to two primary bodies of truth: the resurrection and fulfilled prophecies. We will look at the resurrection later. Several prophecies are of central importance in understanding who Jesus is. First, He was the fulfillment of the prophecy given to King David, that a descendant would sit on David's throne forever. When Jesus said He was king of the Jews, He meant it. He meant He was the Messiah who would reign on the throne of David forever.

"I will raise up your offspring after you", God declared to David through the prophet Nathan, "and I will establish the throne of his kingdom forever. I will be His father and He shall be my Son" (2 Samuel 7:12, 13–14). No Hebrew king had ever fulfilled this prophecy. The Jewish people were waiting for the Messiah, whom they believed would bring this prophecy to fruition. But they were not expecting someone like Jesus. He was so unlike their expectations that many did not believe in Him.

After Samuel, the prophet Isaiah had predicted a more complete picture of the Messiah, whose primary objective, Isaiah said, was to redeem Israel from her sin:

> The Lord himself will give you a sign: Behold, a virgin will be with child and bear a son, and she will call His name Immanuel. Behold, my servant will prosper, He will be high and lifted up, and greatly exalted. Just as many were astonished at you, My people, so His appearance was marred more than any man, and His form more than the sons of men. He was despised and forsaken of

men, a man of sorrows, and acquainted with grief; and like one from whom men hide their face, He was despised, and we did not esteem Him. Surely our griefs He Himself bore, and our sorrows He carried; yet we ourselves esteemed Him stricken, smitten of God, and afflicted. But He was pierced through for our transgressions, He was crushed for our iniquities; the chastening for our well-being fell upon Him, and by His scourging we are healed. All of us like sheep have gone astray, each of us has turned to his own way; but the LORD has caused the iniquity of us all to fall on Him (Isaiah 7:14; 52:13–14; 53:3–6 NASB).

These two prophecies—from Samuel and Isaiah—seem to be contradictory. How can a king, who is high and lifted up be crushed and broken, and have our sin laid on Him? This was so confusing to the Old Testament Jews that one theory of interpretation held that there would be two Messiahs—one who came humble and lowly, to be crushed and broken, and another who would come in power and glory to reign.

Today, we understand these prophecies better in light of New Testament revelations—that Jesus came the first time, humble and lowly to be crushed and broken and die for our sin. After his death, resurrection, and ascension into heaven, He will come again, the second time in power and glory, to reign.

Knowing that Jesus fulfilled these prophecies and will fulfill others when He returns is an essential ingredient in understanding who Jesus is.

Conclusion

Who is Jesus? To answer this question, we will summarize some of the things we have already said, and mention some other truths we will consider in this study.

He is the second member of the Trinity, the Son of God who existed before the world began, and who played an instrumental role in the creation. As God, He had no beginning, and He has no end. He was active in the affairs of men in the Old Testament as the Angel of the Lord, and the Captain of the Hosts of the Lord. He became a human being when he was born to the virgin, Mary, having been miraculously conceived of the Holy Spirit.

Jesus lived a sinless life during a time of cultural upheaval for the Jews, fulfilling the prophecies of the Messiah in his birth, life, death, and resurrection. After a life of three years as an itinerant preacher, he was crucified on false charges brought against him by the Jewish religious leaders. Three days later, He rose from the grave, appeared to a number of people for over a month. Then He ascended into heaven, where He is now, interceding before the throne of God the Father on our behalf. He will come again some day to judge the sin of the world and to establish an eternity of righteousness.

One Solitary Life. This famous but anonymous piece summarizes the importance of Jesus and His great impact on our world in the last two thousand years:

He was born in an obscure village, the child of a peasant woman.

He grew up in still another village, where he worked in a carpenter's shop until he was thirty. Then for three years he was an itinerant preacher.

He never wrote a book. He never held an office. He never had a family or owned a house. He did not go to college. He never visited a big city. He never traveled two hundred miles from the place where he was born. He did none of the things one usually associates with greatness.

He had no credentials but Himself.

He was only thirty-three when the tide of public opinion turned against him. His friends ran away. He was turned over to his enemies and went through the mockery of a trial. He was nailed to a cross between two thieves. While he was dying, his executioners gambled for his clothing, the only property he had on earth. When he was dead, he was laid in a borrowed grave through the pity of a friend.

Nineteen centuries [and now, nearly twenty] have come and gone, and today he remains the central figure of the human race, and the leader of mankind's progress. All the armies that ever marched, all the navies that ever sailed, all the parliaments that ever sat, all the kings that ever reigned, put together, have not affected the life of man on this planet so much as that one solitary life.

This is an amazing tribute. It seems overstated, to claim that one person could have a greater impact on this world than the combined armies, navies, parliaments, and kings of history. Yet, I believe that when the truth about Jesus is known and understood this statement is altogether appropriate and true.

Speed Bump!

Slow down long enough to be sure you've gotten the main points of this chapter.

Question   **Q1.** What do you mean when you say "Jesus"?   ②

Answer   **A1.** Jesus of Nazareth is the *divine* Son of God, the second member of the Trinity, and the Savior of humankind.
② LORD of All who Believe!

Q2. Why believe Jesus was God?

A2. We believe Jesus was God because the *Scriptures* declare Him to be God, and His words and works prove Him to be God.

Q3. Why believe Jesus was a man?

A3. We believe Jesus was a man because the *Scriptures* declare Him to be a man, and His words and works prove Him to be a man.

Fill In the Blank

Question   **Q1.** What do you mean when you say "Jesus"?

Answer   **A1.** Jesus of Nazareth is the _____ Son of God, the second member of the Trinity, and the savior of humankind.

Q2. Why believe Jesus was God?

A2. We believe Jesus was God because the _____ declare Him to be God, and His words and works prove Him to be God.

Q3. Why believe Jesus was a man?

A3. We believe Jesus was a man because the _____ declare Him to be a man, and His words and works prove Him to be a man.

For Further Discussion and Thought

1. If someone were to come up to you on the street and ask you who Jesus was, what would you say?

2. Do you agree with the concept of Jesus as the "Great Rescuer"? If you do, in what ways do you think He is able to rescue humankind?

3. Is there anyone in history you think comes close to being as important as Jesus? Why or why not?

4. How do you think your family experience, educational experience, and other experiences affected your concept of who Jesus is? Do you feel your understanding is better now, or the same?

What If I Don't Believe?

1. I must come up with an explanation for Jesus. He is the single most unusual and important figure in history. What could possibly explain His impact on people and historical events?

2. I must explain away the prophecies which He fulfilled.

3. I must explain why so many people for two thousand years have considered Him divine.

4. I must accept that the Bible is a pack of lies.

5. I must accept that mere humans wrote a book so unlike anything that has ever been written, and so far above anything else ever written that it stands as the dominant publication in history.

For Further Study

1. Scriptures
Several Scripture passages speak of who Jesus is:

- Luke 2:52

- Matthew 16:13–18

- John 20:25–28

- Isaiah 52:13–53:6

- Revelation 4 and 5

Read these passages and consider how they add to your understanding of who God is.

2. Books

There are several other books which are very helpful in studying this subject. They are listed below in general order of difficulty. If I could read only one of these, I would read the first one:

No Wonder They Call Him Savior, Max Lucado
Know What You Believe, Paul Little
Concise Theology, James I. Packer
The Words and Works of Jesus Christ, J. Dwight Pentecost

*You ought to beware thinking that Christ will
achieve things in the earth quietly and softly
when you see that He fought with His own
blood, and afterward with all the martyrs.*
■ Martin Luther

What Is Jesus Like?

Michael Green has written a marvelous little volume titled *Who
Is This Jesus?* Regarding the question of what Jesus was like, he wrote,

One thing is certain. The Jesus who meets us in the pages of the
four Gospels (the accounts of Jesus written by His friends) is very
different from the picture many have of Him. He is nothing like the
"gentle Jesus meek and mild" of the children's stories. He is not the
miserable holy man who never laughs. He is not the fearsome judge
who watches to see if we are enjoying ourselves and then tells us to
stop. Nor is He the lifeless figure in the stained-glass window. Jesus, as
the Gospels reveal Him to us, is radiantly alive and supremely attrac-
tive.

There is a great deal we would love to know that we simply are not
told. We do not even know what He looked like. He was a Palestinian
Jew, and as such the color of His skin would be olive, His eyes brown,
and His nose hooked. Palestinian Jews had black hair and usually wore
it long and carefully groomed. They valued a full beard, and it appears
on many of the coins of the day. His mother tongue was Aramaic, a di-
alect of Hebrew, which He would have spoken with a northern accent
common to Galilee where He was brought up. But He could speak
Greek and probably some Latin and was thoroughly at home in the Hebrew Scriptures. He wore a sleeveless undergarment with a girdle, the
customary cloak and sandals, and carried a staff on journeys. That is all
we know about His appearance or can guess with confidence.

But the Gospels have no interest in these things. They are profoundly disinterested in these things. They are profoundly disinterested in His size, the color of His eyes and hair, and even His age and
strength. These external things are unimportant. What a man is like
stems from his character. And here the Gospels are eloquent. (8–9)

How true! The Gospels talk little about what Jesus looked like, but they tell much about His character. And one characteristic of Jesus dominates: love. True, when you read of Jesus giving a scolding to some religious leaders or driving dishonest money changers out of the temple, love does not seem to be His preeminent characteristic. However, His very presence on earth as God in human form is the greatest act of love ever committed.

The Gospels,

the first four books of the New Testament, record the life of Jesus of Nazareth. They are the books of Matthew, Mark, Luke and John. While none include the name of its writer, ancient and reliable tradition identifies each closely with the disciple of Jesus after whom each is named. (Luke, the only non-Jew among them, became a follower of Jesus after the birth of the Christian church.) Since each writer had a slightly different perspective on Jesus and a different purpose in writing about Him, each book differs somewhat from the others.

Jesus came to earth to love us with profound, unconditional love, and in loving us, to draw us to Himself. When we ask, "What is Jesus like?" we start with, "He loves us." And in loving us, He helps us become all we can be in Him.

Jesus taught that love was the greatest thing in life. Mother Teresa once said,

Spread love everywhere you go: first of all in your own house. Give love to your children, to your wife or husband, to a next door neighbor. . . . Let no one ever come to you without leaving better and happier. Be the living expression of God's kindness; kindness in your face, kindness in your eyes, kindness in your smile, kindness in your warm greeting.

This kind of love has to pervade the human soul. It's not an act. Rather, it springs from the innermost regions of the soul. We may

---

In this chapter we learn that . . .

1. Jesus possessed all the attributes of a man while never giving up any attributes of God.
2. Jesus was subject to the Father because, while all members of the Godhead are equal, they have distinct roles. In the eternal relationships within the Trinity, God the Father has always been in loving authority and Jesus has always been in loving submission.
3. Jesus was a powerful presence who elicited either acceptance or rejection of Him.

value this kind of love, we may admire it when we see it, we may even manifest it now and then. But this kind of love requires the remaking of one's heart.

This kind of love powerfully and dramatically affects those who receive it. Jack Canfield and Mark Hansen in *Chicken Soup for the Soul* tell of a college professor who once had his sociology class go into the Baltimore slums to get case histories of two hundred young boys and to evaluate their futures.

In every case the students wrote, "He hasn't got a chance." Twenty-five years later another sociology professor came across the earlier study. He had his students follow up on the project to see what happened to these boys. With the exception of twenty boys who had moved away or died, the students learned that 176 of the remaining 180 had achieved more than ordinary success as lawyers, doctors and businessmen.

The professor was astounded and decided to pursue the matter further. Fortunately, all the men were in the area and he was able to ask each one, "How do you account for your success?" In each case the reply came with feeling, "There was a teacher."

The teacher was still alive, so he sought her out and asked the old but still alert lady what magic formula she had used to pull these boys out of the slums into successful achievement.

The teacher's eyes sparkled and her lips broke into a gentle smile. "It's really very simple," she said. "I loved those boys" (3–4).

I am persuaded that love is the most powerful force on earth. The behavior even of animals often portrays this. For example, my wife and I used to have a large, black standard poodle. Sugar Bear was a happy dog, for several years part of our lives. Pleasant, loving, and friendly, she was well integrated into the human world. Everyone who knew her loved her.

In a salvage yard a few miles away, a pit bull bared its fangs from behind the chain-link fence whenever a person came within eyesight. Wildness and hatred glared from its eyes, and saliva would drip from its jowls as it snarled and snapped its warning not to come any closer.

What was the difference between those two dogs? Well, some temperament, for sure, because of the differences between the two breeds. But the biggest difference was abundant, loving, and direct contact with human beings. Had the pit bull had the amount of love showered on it that Sugar Bear had on her, I am sure it would have been quite a different dog. Is not the same true with people?

Love is the most powerful force on earth. It can turn enemies into friends, and friends into kindred spirits. Love can stop wars, heal wounded relationships, give meaning to life, and cause personalities to blossom. Ghandi and Martin Luther King Jr. both advocated non-violent social change. They realized that their movements had to be non-violent because they were combating outside forces stronger than they were. And they understood that what you give out, you get back. If you give out violence, you get violence back, and if you are struggling against someone stronger than you, you end up defeated. Their only hope lay in slaying their enemies with love. And in both cases it worked: Love won the day.

All this helps us understand what Jesus is like. When someone asked Him, "Teacher, which is the great commandment in the law?" Jesus replied, "You shall love the Lord your God with all your heart, with all your soul, and with all your mind. This is the first and great commandment. And a second is like it: You shall love your neighbor as yourself." He not only taught this, but He also demonstrated it by example. As we see how He lived, we receive the full impact of His words.

What Was Jesus Like, Being Both God and Man?

Jesus possessed all the attributes of a man while never giving up any attributes of God.

Because of His great love for us, He willingly gave up His position and comfort in heaven to come to earth, live a very difficult life, and eventually die for us. We saw in chapter 1 that Jesus is God and that He existed before He came to earth as Jesus of Nazareth. John 3:16 says, "For God so loved the world that He gave His only begotten Son, that whoever believes in Him should not perish but have everlasting life." Jesus came as God, but also as man, to provide a way for us to be forgiven of our sins, and to have abundant and eternal life. As we understand more of what it means for Jesus to be both God and man, we begin to see the great beauty of His soul. Jesus is altogether lovely, and nothing brings that out more clearly than seeing what He as God relinquished to become man.

When theologians talk about the combining of divinity with humanity, they use the word "kenosis" to describe what happened. "Kenosis" comes from a Greek word (the language in which the New Testament was originally written) which means "to empty." It appears in Philippians 2:3–11. Read this powerful passage with reverence, for in it is reflected one of the most towering callings of humanity.

> Do nothing from selfishness or empty conceit, but with humility of mind let each of you regard one another as more important than himself; do not merely look out for your own personal interests, but also for the interests of others. Have this attitude in yourselves which was also in Christ Jesus, who, although He existed in the form of God, did not regard equality with God a thing to be grasped, but *emptied* Himself, taking the form of a bondservant, and being made in the likeness as a man, He humbled Himself by becoming obedient to the point of death, even death on a cross. Therefore, God also highly exalted Him, and bestowed on Him the name which is above every name, that at the name of Jesus every knee should bow, of those who are in heaven, and on earth, and under the earth, and that every tongue should confess that Jesus Christ is Lord, to the glory of God the Father (emphasis added, NASB).

Imagine! Jesus was God. He lived in eternity past in the glory of heaven. His life was unending perfection. In humble obedience to the Father this Person left His home in heaven, came to earth, took on a human body, lived a difficult life in obedience to God

---

Why I need to know what Jesus is like

If I don't understand what Jesus is like, I will have an inadequate ability to know Him and appreciate Him. I will have an inadequate understanding of how much He loves me and how much He has done for me. I will not be in a position to be changed by Him to the degree that I would if I understood more fully what He is like.

---

the Father, and finally died on the Cross for us. As a result, the Father has exalted Jesus above every other being, giving this God-man the sacred Name of God—LORD—and purposing, in His time, to reveal the exalted Jesus to all of creation as undisputed Lord over all.

Theologians have debated this passage and its implications for the last two thousand years. Many false conclusions have been made about Jesus. People tend to fall into one of two imbalances: to conclude that He was really God and not really human;

or to conclude that He was really human and not really God. Historic Christian teaching, however, has always held that He was fully God and fully human at the same time, without becoming some kind of third being. Even those who believe this have trouble keeping their balance sometimes. In our desire to emphasize the humanness of Jesus, we may water down His deity. Or, in an attempt to underscore His deity, we may dilute His humanity. We must do neither. We must believe that, at the same time, He was fully God and fully man, the only God-man ever to have existed.

However, what does it mean that Christ "emptied" Himself? That is the real question with the "kenosis" doctrine. Did He empty himself of some or of all aspects of deity? If He did, He ceased to be fully God. If He did not, what does "emptied" mean?

"Emptied" may be a misleading translation. The *New International Version* translates the passage, "he made himself nothing." When we look only at these words, we might have difficulty understanding what they mean. However, reading on, the passage itself clarifies the word. It means, first, that He took on the form of a servant. Jesus did not come as a pompous tyrant, but rather as a humble servant. Mark 10:45 says, "For even the Son of Man did not come to be served, but to serve, and to give His life a ransom for many."

So the first thing "emptied" Himself means is that, as God, He came to earth as a servant even though He had every right to come as a sovereign. Second, in "being made in likeness as a man," He did not come to earth in a human rent-a-body that He used for thirty some years and then discarded He did not come as the Angel of the Lord, He did not come as some unique celestial being. But He became a man, born of a woman, with a permanent, fully human body. Finally, He humbled Himself and played out the role which God the Father chose for Him.

Jesus was and is the only God-man: fully God and fully man.

Jesus, then, gave up nothing of His deity. He just took on humanity. Often, those who water down His deity say that He was not omniscient (all-knowing), or omnipotent (all-powerful) or omnipresent (everywhere present), yet the Bible makes it clear that He possessed these attributes during the time of His life on earth (Matthew 18:20; 28:18; Mark. 2:8). How? Because He is able to do things which humans can't. In fact, He is able to do things that humans can't even understand.

How, then, can we describe what the "kenosis" was? It involves these actions:

1. His pre-incarnate glory was veiled: that is, the glory that He had before He came to earth was veiled by His human form. One time, Jesus went up on a mountain with three of His disciples, Peter, James, and John. While they were there, Jesus suddenly changed His appearance.

Jesus did not come to earth in a human rent-a-body that He used for thirty years and then discarded.

Mark 9:23 says, "and He was transfigured before them. His clothes became shining, exceedingly white like snow, such as no launderer on earth can whiten them." In a passage in Matthew describing the same event, we read that "His face shone like the sun, and His clothes became as white as the light" (17:2). In another passage, after Jesus' crucifixion, Mary and Mary Magdalene went to the grave where He had been buried. "And behold, there was a great earthquake; for an angel of the Lord descended from heaven, and came and rolled back the stone from the door, and sat upon it. His countenance was like lightning, and his clothing as white as snow" (Matthew 28:2–3).

Now, this was not Jesus; it was an angel. But from these and other passages, it appears that "standard issue" bodies in heaven appear as though they have been carved out of a lightning bolt or a piece of the noon-day sun. For obvious reasons, Jesus did not walk around like that during His earthly ministry. He veiled the glory of His true self.

2. He voluntarily did not use some of His divine attributes some of the time (Matthew 24:36). Nonuse does not mean subtraction. Just because He didn't use them doesn't mean He didn't have them, or could not have used them if He had chosen.

That is what "kenosis" means. That is what it means when it says "He emptied Himself." He voluntarily veiled His divine glory, and He did not use some of His attributes some of the time. Instead, He took on human form, humbled Himself to the plan of God the Father, and died on the Cross for our sins.

What a beautiful person He is! What kindness! What sacrifice! What unfathomable love!

Why Was Jesus Subject to God the Father?

Jesus was subject to the Father because, while all members of the Godhead are equal, they have distinct roles in their saving activity toward humanity. God the Father has always been in loving authority, and Jesus has always been in loving submission.

To better understand what Jesus is like we must understand His relationship with God the Father. There is only one God, but the one God exists as three eternal and co-equal Persons, the same in substance, but distinct in subsistence.

Though the three members of the Godhead are equal, they have different roles to play in their saving activity toward humanity. God the Father is the authority in the Godhead, and Jesus fulfills the will of the Father. Yet, the Father's intent is to exalt the Son. That shows the perfect basis of relationship if conflict is to be avoided and unity experienced. One is in authority, the other serves that authority, yet the one in authority has as His intent to exalt the one under authority. It is a celestial "mutual admiration society" (John 17:1–5).

This explains why God has established husband and wife relationships the way He has. In fact all relationships that are part of the fabric of any society should be "authority/submission" relationships, with the one under authority submitting to the one in authority, and the one in authority serving the needs of the one in submission, and looking for ways to exalt the one in submission. Whether it is government and citizen, church and member, husband and wife, parent and child, or employer and employee, the governing principle is the same. The one in authority is to use his authority benevolently, for the good of those under him; and the one under him responds with respect and a servant's heart.

Authority and submission within the Trinity provide the basis for human relationships of authority and submission.

God established earthly relationships this way, not because He wanted to keep any element of society under control, but because He wanted all the world to experience the peace, the love, the joy, and the unity of purpose and person that exists in the Trinity. He wanted humanity to experience a likeness to God, to the degree that is possible for finite beings. It was for good, and not for evil, that the Lord established the authority-and-submission pattern in creation. The sinfulness of humanity has perverted the original design, and turned that which is good into something bad.

What is Jesus like?

Jesus is a very powerful person, with great authority. But all His power, all His authority, and His very "person" are under the authority of God the Father. He is one in authority, and under authority, and comfortable with both. As our example, He shows us the way to live, even in a sinful world where people do not rule over us benevolently, as the Father does the Son.

In 1 Peter 2:18–24, we read of the example of this gentle soul who is our pattern for life:

> Servants, be submissive to your masters with all fear, not only to the good and gentle, but also to the harsh. For this is commendable, if because of conscience toward God one endures grief, suffering wrongfully. For what credit is it if, when you are beaten for your faults, you take it patiently? But when you do good and suffer, if you take it patiently, this is commendable before God. For to this you were called, because Christ also suffered for us, leaving us an example that we should follow His steps; "who committed no sin, nor was deceit found in His mouth" who, when He was reviled, did not revile in return; when He suffered, He did not threaten, but committed Himself to Him who judges righteously; who Himself bore our sins in His own body on the tree, that we having died to sins, might live for righteousness—by whose stripes you were healed.

This is what Jesus was like. And this is what we are to be like.

How Did Jesus Influence Others?

Jesus' powerful presence moved people either to accept or reject Him.

Part of the "veiling" of Jesus' glory during His time on earth had to do with the voluntary non-use of some of His divine abilities some of the time. Luke 2:52 says that "Jesus increased in wisdom and stature, and in favor with God and men." I think this means that Jesus chose to grow up as other children did. He memorized Scripture so that when He quoted it, He was not quoting it from His divine attribute of omniscience (knowing everything, both actual and possible), but from His human attribute of self-discipline, having studied and memorized the material.

Jesus exerted tremendous influence over others in eight ways:

1. Jesus was also very intelligent, creative, and incisive. Jesus often confounded the intellects of His day. He continually "bumped heads" with the religious leaders. One day, as Jesus was teaching in the temple, the religious leaders were trying to find some way to discredit Him, or better yet, to catch Him in some violation of the Law so that they could really harm Him. They asked Him, "By what authority are You doing these things? Who gave You this authority?" I think they were hoping to have Him say something about God, so they could accuse Him of blaspheming. But in any case, Jesus answered them with a question. "I also will ask you one thing, which if you tell Me, I likewise will tell you by what authority I do these things: The baptism of John—where was it from? From heaven or from men?"

That pitched the religious leaders into confusion. They thought that if they said, "From heaven," Jesus would say, "Then why did not you believe him?" On the other hand, if they answered, "From men," they feared that the people would become angry and disillusioned with them because the people believed John was a prophet. So they answered, "We do not know."

Jesus replied, "Neither will I tell you by what authority I do these things" (Matthew 21:23–27).

2. Jesus was compassionate. Leprosy was, and is, one of the most repulsive of diseases. It monstrously disfigures by eating away its victims' noses, ears, fingers, and toes. They become crippled, tragic distortions of themselves. In biblical times, leprosy could not be treated, so people were terrified of it. In addition to their crippling physical condition, lepers suffered socially as utter outcasts. To give people a chance to get out of their way and prevent contamination, lepers were required to cry "Unclean! Unclean!" as they walked anywhere, so others could keep a safe distance away.

Understanding the plight of lepers makes Jesus' response to a leper truly compassionate. Matthew reports that a man with leprosy came and knelt before Him and said, "Lord, if you are willing, you can make me clean." Jesus reached out his hand and *touched* the man. "I am willing," he said. "Be cleansed!" Immediately he was cured of his leprosy (Matthew 8:2–3).

You just didn't reach out and touch a leper in those days. In fact, if there had been one cardinal rule regarding lepers it would have been, "Don't touch a leper!" Period. Yet Jesus did. Jesus could have healed him with merely a spoken word, but He *touched* him. How long had it been since that man had felt the touch of a "clean" person? How long had it been since his "personhood" had been affirmed by loving contact with normal humanity? Yes, Jesus was God, and that explains a lot. But He was also a giant among men, the greatest man ever to walk this earth. Examples like this support such a statement.

But His compassion did not stop with no-hope diseases. Jesus exhibited great compassion to people who wanted out of their sin. A woman caught in the very act of adultery was brought to Him. The religious leaders wanted to stone her, even though they knew they couldn't because Roman law prohibited them from doing so. So we know it was another of their pathetic ploys to try to trap Jesus. Jesus said, "He who is without sin among you, let him throw a stone at her first." Humiliated by that, all the instigators drifted away, leaving Jesus alone with the woman. Jesus asked, "Woman, where are those accusers of yours? Has no one condemned you?"

She answered, "No one, Lord."

"Neither do I condemn you." Jesus said, "Go and sin no more."

I believe Jesus saw the repentance in her heart and not only forgave her, but made her "feel" forgiven. What great compassion! What a God! What a Man! How kind of Him, to be "kind." How wonderful that He does not huff, fold His arms, and threaten to box our ears when we come to him in faith for forgiveness. Instead, He reaches out to us, and not only forgives us, but makes us "feel" forgiven. He deserves all He asks of us.

3. Jesus was very direct. While Jesus was very patient, understanding, and compassionate with those with weaknesses, He was very direct with those who were stubbornly unbelieving. Many times the Bible says that the religious leaders did not believe in Jesus because they were jealous of Him. He challenged their pride of position and prestige over the people. Jesus was not patient with these leaders and was very forthright in His responses to them.

These religious leaders observed many customs and traditions that often violated Scripture. For example, they had elaborate rituals for washing utensils and dishes from which they ate. In one confrontation with them, Jesus said, "Woe to you, scribes and Pharisees, hypocrites! For you cleanse the outside of the cup and dish, but inside they are full of extortion and self-indulgence. Blind Pharisee, first cleanse the inside of the cup and dish, that the outside of them may be clean also" (Matthew 23:25–26).

He was saying that their personal lives were clean on the outside, but not on the inside. Today, it would be considered impolite and going overboard to speak in this way to any religious leader, and perhaps so. But Jesus being God saw the true nature of their hearts and had the moral authority to speak so directly. He was not one to trifle with if you were deliberately cooperating with sin.

4. Jesus had great charisma. He attracted huge crowds. People endangered themselves to get near Him. People pressed upon Him so forcefully that He sometimes had to escape. He crossed all social, economic, and political barriers, as people with great charisma often do. I mention Ghandi and Martin Luther King, Jr., not to compare them fully with Jesus, who, as God, outstrips any comparison. But they, like Jesus, were brilliant and gifted, yet comfortable with kings and commoners alike. In Jesus' case, religious leaders, political leaders, common laborers, tax gatherers, homemakers, and prostitutes all felt comfortable in His company and sought Him out.

His words stirred the simple and the sophisticated, the unschooled and the educated. He might rebuke a prominent religious leader one moment, and lift a little child in His arms to bless him the next. He held tens of thousands of people spellbound at a time, yet could talk warmly one-on-one. His words have lasted two thousand years, yet they have the same effect now as they did then. His charisma did not cease with the grave, but lives yet today in His written words.

5. Jesus' life was compelling. Not only was Jesus a man of great charisma, be it with one man or ten thousand, but He lived so completely. He never sinned. He never misspoke. He never acted unbecomingly or was selfish, arrogant, or rude. He could have had great wealth and power, yet He turned them aside, counting them as nothing. He showed kindness to the wounded, fed the hungry, counselled the confused, and broke the chains of demonic slavery. Yet in it all, He took nothing for Himself. He lived and died in poverty and social disapproval. Had Jesus been out to serve Himself, He could easily have done so. The total absence of any act of selfishness in His life is compelling in itself, and lends great power and authority to His words.

6. Jesus spoke with great authority. Lewis Sperry Chafer, founder of Dallas Theological Seminary, once wrote that the Bible was not the kind of book that man would write if he could, or could write if he would. How true. Jesus' teachings were so dramatic, so unexpected, so contrary to human nature that His listeners were continually enthralled, surprised, and transfixed. He taught that the law of love was supreme, that we were to do unto others as we would have other do unto us. He peeled back layers of custom and tradition to expose the heart of the law: that a man would not harm his neighbor.

He insisted that it was not enough not to commit adultery; we were not even to look on a woman with lust in our heart. Not only were we not to murder, we were not even to hate. When He was speaking to a crowd in the Gospel of Mark, the response was, "They were astonished at His teaching, for He taught them as one having authority, and not as the scribes" (Mark 1:22). When Jesus spoke, He never footnoted His contemporaries. He never said, "As Rabbi Hillel once said, etc." He always quoted the Old Testament or used His own words. His inner power and authority came through to the people as He taught them.

7. Jesus was a man of dramatic action. Publicly, Jesus verbally whiplashed the religious leaders whose teachings were leading the masses astray. He strode into the temple, turned over tables, set loose livestock, and evacuated the riff raff who were cheating the public and making illicit money on the obligatory temple activities. He called a man back from the dead after four days in the grave. He stilled storms and divided a few loaves and fish to feed thousands of people. He cast demons out of men feared far and wide for their wildness, and later communed with them. The drama of the events of Jesus' life is unmatched by any other human being's. He astonished the public, and as a result, when He spoke, everyone listened.

8. Jesus was a free man. Few things are more powerful than a man who does not fear death. When it doesn't matter whether you live or die, but you will do what is good and right and true, you are a free man. You are free of fear, free of temptation, free of corruption, free of lust, greed, and arrogance. You are free. When Pilate was questioning Him before His crucifixion, Jesus refused to answer him. Pilate said, "Why do you refuse to answer me? Don't you realize I have the power of life and death over you?" Jesus calmly replied, "You have no power except that which has been given to you by My heavenly Father."

He died at the age of thirty-three, not because He miscalculated the political climate, not because His army was too small, not because He was overpowered by those greater than He. He died because, according to the plan of God the Father, the time was right, and He laid down His own life. "No one has taken it from Me, but I lay it down of myself. I have power to lay it down, and I have power to take it up again. This command I have received from My Father" (John 10:18).

What was Jesus like? Like no other man who ever lived before Him, like no other man who has lived since, like no other man who ever will live.

Conclusion

Dr. S. M. Lockridge, a pastor from Dallas, Texas, in a sermon titled "Amen" did his best to describe what Jesus was like:

My king was born king. The Bible says He is the seven-way king. He is the king of the Jews. That's a racial king. He is king of Israel. That's a national king. He's a king of righteousness. He's a king of the ages. He's the king of heaven. He is the king of glory. He's the King of kings and Lord of lords. Now that's my king.

Well, I wonder if you know Him. Do you know Him? Don't try to mislead me. Do you know my king? David said, "The heavens declare the glory of God and the firmament showeth His handiwork." No far-seeing telescope can bring into visibility the coastline of His shoreless supply. No barriers can hinder Him from pouring out His blessing.

He's enduringly strong, He's entirely sincere, He's eternally steadfast. He's immortally graceful. He's imperially powerful. He's impartially merciful. That's my king. He's God's Son. He's a sinner's savior. He's the centerpiece of civilization. He stands alone in Himself. He's august. He's unique. He's unparalleled. He's unprecedented. He's supreme. He's preeminent. He's the loftiest idea in literature. He's the highest idea in philosophy. He's the fundamental truth in theology. He's the cardinal necessity of spiritual religion. That's my king.

He's the miracle of the age. He's the only one able to supply all of our needs simultaneously. He supplies strength for the weak. He's available for the tempted and the **Do you know my king?** tried. He sympathizes and He saves. He guards and He guides. He heals the sick, He cleans the lepers, He forgives sinners, He discharges debtors, He delivers captives, He defends the feeble, He blesses the young, He serves the unfortunate, He regards the aged, He rewards the diligent, He beautifies the meek. Do you know Him?

Well, my king is the king of knowledge, He's the well-spring of wisdom, He's the doorway of deliverance, He's the pathway of peace, He's the roadway of righteousness, He's the highway of holiness, He's the gateway of glory, He's the master of the mighty, He's the captain of the conquerors, He's the head of the heroes, He's the leader of the legislators, He's the overseer of the overcomers, He's the governor of governors, He's the prince of princes, He's the king of Kings and the Lord of Lords. That's my king. Yeah! That's my king.

His life is matchless. His goodness is limitless. His mercy is everlasting. His love never changes. His word is enough. His grace is sufficient. His reign is righteous. His yoke is easy and His burden is light. Well. I wish I could describe Him to you. But He's indescribable. He's indescribable. Yes. He's incomprehensible. He's invincible, He's irresistible. I'm trying to tell you, the Heavens cannot contain Him, let alone a man explain Him. You can't get Him out of your mind. You can't get Him off of your hands. You can't outlive Him, and you can't live without Him. Well. The Pharisees couldn't stand Him, but they found out they couldn't stop Him. Pilate couldn't find any fault in Him. The witnesses [at his trial] couldn't get their testimonies to agree. Herod couldn't kill Him. Death couldn't handle Him and the grave couldn't hold Him. That's my king. Yeah!

He always has been, and He always will be. I'm talking about He [who] had no predecessor and He [who] has no successor.

There was nobody before Him and there will be nobody after Him. You can't impeach Him, and He's not going to resign. Praise the Lord! That's my king. Thine is the kingdom and the power and the glory. Well. All the power belongs to my king. We around here talk about black power and white power and green power, but it's God's power. Thine is the power. Yeah! And the glory. We try to get prestige and honor and glory to ourselves, but the glory is all His. Thine is the kingdom *and* the power *and* the glory forever, and ever, and ever, and ever. How long is that? And ever, and ever, and ever, and ever, and when you get through with all of the forevers, then "Amen."

Speed Bump!

Slow down to make sure you've gotten the main points of this chapter.

Question
Answer

Q1. What was Jesus like, being both God and man?

A1. Jesus possessed all the attributes of a man, while never *giving up* any attributes of God.

Q2. Why was Jesus subject to God the Father?

A2. Jesus was subject to the Father because, while all members of the Godhead are equal, they have distinct *roles*, in their saving activity toward humanity God the Father has always been in loving authority and Jesus has always been in loving submission.

Q3. How did Jesus influence others?

A3. Jesus' *powerful* presence moved people either to accept or reject Him.

Fill In the Blank

Question
Answer

Q1. What was Jesus like, being both God and man?

A1. Jesus possessed all the attributes of a man while never _____ any attributes of God.

Q2. Why was Jesus subject to God the Father?

A2. Jesus was subject to the Father because, while all members of the Godhead are equal, they have distinct _____ and in their saving activity toward humanity God the Father has always been in loving authority and Jesus has always been in loving submission.

Q3. How did Jesus influence others?

A3. Jesus' _____ presence moved people either to accept or reject Him.

For Further Thought and Discussion

1. If someone had asked you before you read this chapter what Jesus was like, what would you have said? What would you say now that you have read this chapter? Has your impression changed? If so, how?

2. If you were to rate your understanding of how much God loves you, and how much you have perceived that love, would you be more like Sugar Bear or the junkyard dog? If you could gain a fuller understanding of God's love, do you think it would change you?

3. Explain, to the best of your own understanding and in your own words, what "kenosis" means.

4. What lessons do you think Jesus' example of submission to the Father teach you?

5. What do you think your response to Jesus would be if you had lived when he did and heard Him preach and witness His ministry?

What If I Don't Believe?

1. If I don't believe that Jesus was both God and man, I lose whatever I don't believe. If I don't believe He was God, I lose someone who could save me, because of His divine perfection. If I don't believe He was a man, I lose someone who can save me because no one with divine perfection is available to die in my place, which is what God requires for my salvation.

2. If I don't believe that Jesus' dominant motivating characteristic is love for me, I have a diminished view of who He is and what He has done for me. As a result, I don't feel loved by Him, and stand a greater chance of turning out like the junkyard dog than Sugar Bear.

3. If I don't believe that Jesus was in willing submission to God the Father, I lose the power of the example of submission in love. I lose my understanding of how relationships in the Trinity work, and therefore,

how relationships on earth must work. I also lose some of the power of the lesson that I need to be in submission to God.

For Further Study

1. Scripture Passages
A number of passages are important to our understanding of what Jesus is like. They include:

- Matthew 22:37–40

- Philippians 2:3–11

- John 17:1–4

- 1 Peter 2:18–24

2. Books
There are several other books which are very helpful in studying this subject. They are listed below in general order of difficulty. If I could read only one of these, I would read the first one:

The Master, John Pollock
No Wonder They Call Him Savior, Max Lucado
The Words and Works of Jesus Christ, J. Dwight Pentecost

The love of our neighbor is the only door out
of the dungeon of self.
■ **George MacDonald**

3

What Did Jesus Teach?

once read a story which reminded me of Jesus the teacher:

I was driving to a business appointment and, as usual, I was planning in my mind what I was going to say. I came to a very busy intersection where the stoplight had just turned red. "All right," I thought to myself, "I can beat the next light if I race ahead of the pack."

My mind and car were on autopilot, ready to go when suddenly my trance was broken by an unforgettable sight. A young couple, both blind, were walking arm-in-arm across this busy intersection with cars whizzing by in every direction. The man was clutching the hand of a little boy, while the woman was clutching a baby sling to her chest, obviously carrying a child. Each of them had a white cane extended, searching for clues to navigate them across the intersection.

Initially I was moved. They were overcoming what I felt was one of the most feared handicaps—blindness. "Wouldn't it be terrible to be blind?" I thought. My thought was quickly interrupted by horror when I saw that the couple were not walking in the crosswalk, but were instead veering diagonally, directly toward the middle of the intersection. Without realizing the danger they were in, they were walking right smack into the path of oncoming cars. I was frightened for them because I didn't know if the other drivers understood what was happening.

As I watched from the front line of traffic (I had the best seat in the house), I saw a miracle unfold before my eyes. *Every* car in *every* direction came to a simultaneous stop. I never heard the screech of brakes or even the peep of a car horn. Nobody even yelled, "Get out of the way!" Everything froze. In that moment, time seemed to stand still for this family.

Amazed, I looked at the cars around me to verify that we were all seeing the same thing. I noticed that everyone's attention was fixed on the couple. Suddenly the driver to my right reacted. Craning his head out of his car, he yelled, "To your right. To your right!" Other people followed in unison, shouting, "To your right!"

Never skipping a beat, the couple adjusted their course as they followed the coaching. Trusting their white canes and the calls from some concerned citizens, they made it to the other side of the road. As they arrived at the curb, one thing struck me—they were still arm in arm.

I was taken aback by the emotionless expressions on their faces and judged that they had no idea what was really going on around them. Yet I immediately sensed the sighs of relief exhaled by everyone stopped at that intersection.

As I glanced into the cars around me, the driver on my right was mouthing the words "Whew, did you see that?" The driver to the left of me was saying, "I can't believe it!" I think all of us were deeply moved by what we had just witnessed. Here were human beings stepping outside themselves for a moment to help four people in need (*Chicken Soup for the Soul*, 284–285).

The spirit in which the drivers at that intersection guided the blind couple is the spirit in which Jesus came to guide humanity. The drivers looked at the blind couple in terrible danger and their hearts went out to them. With significant emotional investment, all those drivers called out "To your right! To your right!"

So it was with Jesus. He came to earth because He loved us. He saw that we were not only lost, we were in danger. However, instead of veering into a perilous zone where we might get hurt, we were marching off a cliff to certain death. He came to warn humanity of sure disaster and to save them from it. He did not teach with the excitement

---

In this chapter we learn that . . .

1. Jesus taught that humanity is spiritually lost and needs to be saved.
2. Jesus taught that true righteousness is internal, not external.
3. Jesus taught that we should love God with all our heart and soul and mind.

---

of a fresh, new teacher eager to impart knowledge he loved to students. He taught with the urgency of all those people trying to keep the blind couple from getting killed. He did not come to say, "Now class, turn to your reading lesson for today. There you will find a story you will greatly enjoy." Rather, he came to shout to humanity, *"To your right! To your right!"*

As a minister and pastor for over twenty years at the time of this writing, I have seen a constant stream of people walking blindly toward a dangerous precipice. Others were calling to them, "To the right! To the right!" Ignoring all warnings, they just kept walking, and fell into terrible trouble they could otherwise easily have avoided. Worse yet, it wrenches your heart to watch someone look right at your warning, but maintain their direction and march right off the cliff. If it breaks my heart . . . if it breaks your heart, think what it does to the heart of God. He is watching a river of humanity pour over the cliff, and for all time. He calls and calls to humanity, but only a few heed the barricades He erected at tremendous cost and turn from destruction.

Yes, Jesus was a teacher. In fact, people commonly called Him "Rabbi." Teacher. But Jesus did not come to teach because He liked teaching. He taught because He loved humanity and was desperate to save it. His words, as relevant today as they were the first time He uttered them, are the subject of this chapter. What did Jesus teach? When He called out "To the right! To the right!" what was He saying to us?

When we categorize Jesus' teachings, we discover that everything fits under one of four basic headings. In this chapter we will look at four primary teachings of Jesus.

1. What Did Jesus Teach About Humanity's Greatest Need?

Jesus taught that humanity is spiritually lost and needs to be saved.

Humanity's greatest need is salvation. Sin separated humankind from God and until the sin was removed, people would be separated from God forever.

Jesus' Forerunner

John the Baptist preached hot words of judgment and retribution unless people repented, changed their ways, and prepared their hearts for the coming of the Messiah. "Repent, for the kingdom of heaven is at hand!" he cried. "Make ready the way of the Lord, make His paths straight!" The Gospel of Matthew records that "Jerusalem was going out to him, and all Judea, and all the district around the Jordan; and they were being baptized by him in the Jordan River, as they confessed their sins" (3:5–6 NASB). Think of it. Masses from the major city, masses from the province of Judea, crowds from the area near the Jordan River flocked to hear Him. That is a lot of people. John was a major phenomenon.

His name would have been on the lips of every informed person in that part of the world.

John was very compassionate with the repentant. He didn't scold or berate them. But, oh, how he tore into the religious leaders of the day.

> When he saw many of the Pharisees and Sadducees [the religious leaders of the day] coming for baptism, he said to them, "You brood of vipers [translation: you low-down snakes in the grass], who warned you to flee from the wrath to come? Therefore, bring forth fruit in keeping with your repentance . . . the ax is already laid at the root of the trees; every tree therefore, that does not bear good fruit is cut down and thrown into the fire" [if you do not repent of your sins, God has already determined that you will be judged!] (Matthew 3:7–8, 10 NASB).

No one had ever dared to speak to these men like that. They were the elite in their communities. They were the "movers and shakers" of their nation. "If you are righteous, prove it by your deeds, not just by the act of being baptized," John was saying. Being a Jew was not good enough. Visiting the temple, observing the feasts, and participating in the local synagogue was not good enough. Inner cleansing was the issue. God requires genuine repentance from sin, and turning to true righteousness. The Messiah is soon to come, and since He also will require repentance, get ready now. Get your hearts ready for the coming of God to earth. That was the message of John the Baptist.

Humanity's greatest need is to be rescued from spiritual death.

After John was arrested for publicly denouncing the adultery of Herod, the local ruler of that area, Jesus appeared on the scene. "Now after John had been taken into custody [had been arrested], Jesus came into Galilee, preaching the gospel of God, and saying, 'The time is fulfilled, and the kingdom of God is at hand; repent and believe in the gospel'" (Mark 1:14–15 NASB). His message was the same. The kingdom of God is at hand. Get your hearts ready.

Jesus and Nicodemus

Later, Jesus clarified all this. After He had been ministering for a short time, he caught the attention of a man named Nicodemus, a very prominent religious leader. Nicodemus came to Jesus by night (maybe he was too busy in the daytime, or perhaps he wanted to keep his meeting with Jesus a secret for fear of what the other religious leaders would say). He said to Jesus, "Rabbi, we know that You have come from God as a teacher, for no one can do these signs [referring to Jesus' miracles] that You do unless God is with him." Jesus replied "Nicodemus, you need to be born again." Nicodemus was flummoxed. Born again? What did *that* mean? Jesus went on, "For God so loved the world that He gave His only begotten Son, that whoever believes in Him should not perish, but have eternal life. For God did not send the Son into the world to judge the world; but that the world should be saved through Him. He who believes in Him is not judged; he who does not believe has been judged already, because he has not believed in the name of the only begotten Son of God" (John 3:2–3, 16–18 NASB).

What amazing statements! Nothing like this had ever been heard in Israel. Jesus revealed His purpose and mission: Unless a person believed in Him (which means committing his life to Him), he was separated from God forever. But Jesus had come so that people would not have to be separated from God forever, but through Him could be reconciled to God.

That is the first thing Jesus taught when He began His ministry, and it is the most important thing He taught. Elsewhere Jesus said, "What does it profit a man if He gains the whole world, but loses his soul?" The obvious answer is "nothing." What did Jesus teach about mankind's greatest need? That mankind was doomed to perish and needed to be saved.

Closely related to this subject was that of Jesus' crucifixion, resurrection, ascension into heaven, and, ultimately, His coming again to judge the world of sin and righteousness. Those who believed in Him and received Him would be rewarded according to their faith, and those who rejected Him would be judged according to their unbelief.

2. What Did Jesus Teach About True Righteousness?

Jesus taught that true righteousness is internal, not external.

So many barnacles of tradition, hypocrisy, injustice, and apathy encrusted the ship of Judaism (the Jewish faith) that, from Jesus' perspective, it threatened to sink. "You teach as law the traditions of men and in doing so, violate the Law!" He charged. In a classic exchange in Matthew 23, Jesus was addressing a large multitude of people which included scribes and Pharisees (religious leaders), and He aimed seven "woes" directly at them, by name. His whole point in denouncing these men was that they kept the traditions of men but did not keep the Law of God. "Woe to you, scribes and Pharisees, hypocrites, because . . .

- you do not enter the kingdom of heaven,
- and by your teachings keep others from entering it,
- you take advantage of disadvantaged people,
- you go to great lengths to find converts, then
- pervert them as you are perverted,
- you keep small parts of the law, but ignore the great part
- you are righteous on the outside, but unrighteous on the inside,
- you appear righteous to men, but are full of hypocrisy and lawlessness,
- you honor past prophets with monuments, but kill present-day prophets."

This is what is known as a "Scathing Rebuke." Jesus called them hypocrites, blind guides, whitewashed tombs, serpents, brood of vipers, and murderers. But for the most part, the rebuke fell on deaf ears.

The Sermon on the Mount

The whole point of Jesus' first and best known major address, the Sermon on the Mount in chapters 5—7 of the Gospel of Matthew, is that true righteousness is internal, not external. If it were external, the Pharisees would have had heaven wrapped up, because on the outside they were as pretty as could be. However, inside they were full of mold and rot. "Unless your righteousness surpasses the righteousness of the scribes and Pharisees, you shall not enter the kingdom of heaven," Jesus said (5:20 NASB).

In stark contrast to the seven woes he pronounced on the scribes and Pharisees, he offered eight beatitudes (blessings) to those who were inwardly righteous.

It is really absurd to live as though we could pull the wool over God's eyes. Do we think we can hoodwink someone who knows all things both actual and possible? What a collapse of logic it is to live one way on the outside, be another way on the

---

The Beatitudes of Jesus

Blessed are those who recognize their deep spiritual needs, for the kingdom of heaven will be theirs.

Blessed are those who are deeply saddened, for they shall be comforted by God.

Blessed are those who have a strong desire to be like God, for God will satisfy their desire.

Blessed are those who show mercy to others, for mercy will be shown to them in return.

Blessed are these who are pure in their motives and desires, for they will be with God.

Blessed are those who work to bring about peace, for they will be sons of God.

Blessed are those who have suffered for doing what is right, for the kingdom of heaven will be theirs.

Blessed are you when people insult you, and treat you badly, and say evil lies about you because you follow Me. Celebrate and be happy, for you will have great reward in heaven. . .

(author's paraphrase, Matthew 5:3–12).

---

inside, and think that God would be pleased. No, God is not vulnerable to spiritual "sleight of hand." True righteousness is internal, not external.

3. What Did Jesus Teach Was the Most Important Commandment?

Jesus taught that we should love God with all our heart and soul and mind.

Jesus was speaking to a group of religious leaders when one of them, a specialist in interpreting the Jewish law, asked Him what the greatest commandment was. He asked Jesus this question to try to trip Him up on an answer somehow. Without hesitation Jesus answered, "You shall love the LORD your God with all your heart, and with all your soul, and with all your mind. This is the great and foremost commandment" (Matthew 22:37–38 NASB).

Our task, then, is to determine what it means to love God. Does it mean to have great swells of emotion race up and down your spine like a finger tripping up and down a piano keyboard? Does it mean to live with goose bumps on the back of your neck?

Does it mean to be filled at all times with warm thoughts of God? What does it mean to love God?

Why I need to know this

People are often very unclear in their understanding of what it means to be a Christian, on who Jesus was, and what He taught and requires of His followers. In a day when so many people consider truth to be relative, and that Jesus can be whatever they want, it is imperative that we know what Jesus says about Himself, what He said a true Christian is, and what He requires of His followers. Truth is what Jesus says it is, regardless of what we think or feel. We need to know what Jesus says is the truth.

To Love God Is a Commandment

In seeking an answer that will work, we must remember that to love God is a commandment. That means we can control whether or not we love God. So we ask ourselves the question, can we control whether or not great swells of emotion constantly tingle our spine? Can we control whether or not goose bumps take up permanent residence on our neck? Can we control whether or not warm, fuzzy thoughts are harbored at all times in the depths our heart? If we can't, then we must exclude any of them in our definition of love. Most of us, because of cultural conditioning, think of love only as an emotion. However, we cannot command emotions. We can command only the will. So, if we are going to come up with an understanding of loving God that will work, it must have to do with the will, not the emotions.

Scripture helps us here. The apostle John, in fact, solves the problem. He writes in the Gospel of John 14:21, 23,

> *He who has My commandments and keeps them, it is he who loves Me.* And he who loves Me will be loved by My Father, and I will love him and will manifest Myself to him. . . . If anyone loves Me, he will keep My word; and My Father will love him, and We will come to him, and make Our home with him (emphasis added).

We see, then, that to love God is to keep His commandments. Not with gritted teeth, but with a trusting heart. Not with clenched fist, but with a sweetly submissive spirit. If we love God, we do as He asks us. Emotions may run up and down our spine, or they may not. It doesn't matter. What matters is that we have obeyed Him. John goes on to write in chapter 15:10–11: "If you keep My commandments, you will abide in My love; just as I have kept My Father's commandments and abide in His love. These things I have spoken to you, that My joy may remain in you, and that your joy may be full."

The Keeping of God's Commandments Brings Joy

That is what these verses are saying. The links go like this: If you love God, you will keep His commandments. If you keep His commandments, you will experience joy. What a revelation! That is the exact opposite of most people's concept of obeying God. We fear that if we obey God, our life will be joyless. "Oh, God, puleeze don't send me to deepest, darkest Africa!" we plead when we come close to selling out to God. We feel the relentless pull of the Holy Spirit in us, convicting us of our sin (our half-hearted pursuit of God), and calling us to righteousness. But, visions of dense jungles, slithering snakes, spiders, and poisonous toads dance into our minds. *If I become completely obedient to God, He will ask me to do the one thing I hate*, we reason; and going to Africa seems to head the list of dreaded things.

Let me tell you. I have known people who gave their lives completely in obedience to God, and He did send them to deepest, darkest Africa. And do you know what? They would rather be in deepest, darkest Africa than any place else on earth. That is the one place they feel at home. When they come home for furlough, they are not here for long before they begin to long for Africa!

On the other hand, only the smallest handful of people I know who have sold themselves out to total obedience to God have ended up in Africa. They usually end up doing the one thing they would rather do than anything else. Some of them pastor. Others are chaplains in the army. Some are traveling evangelists. But by far, most of them are businessmen, laborers, executives, homemakers, educators and the like. If it is true that obeying God is the pathway to joy, He would not send you somewhere that you will be miserable the rest of your life. Those two things don't go together.

Do you want to love God? Obey Him. Do you disobey God? Then to the degree you do not obey Him, you don't love Him. None of us loves God without fail. I don't want to put a guilt trip on you and suggest that if you do not obey God in all things, you do not love Him at all. That is incorrect. It is always a matter of degrees. We obey Him none of the time, or some of the time, or much of the time, or most of the time. (Circle one.) And to that degree, we love God. Do you have emotions sweeping up and down your soul? Wonderful. God has wired you with much emotion. Do you have stainless steel in your spine, which rarely accommodates emotion? Wonderful. God has wired you with cool, steady evenness. The world needs both. They are often married to each other.

But don't be fooled into either of the two most obvious errors: first, assuming that you love God because you feel deep emotions about Him, or readily feel His presence, or are moved greatly during worship services. Those are not the marks of love for God. Those are simply the results of your personal emotional make-up. When you leave that church service, you may go home to a live-in boyfriend, or to a job where you do unethical things, or to a family that you treat with contempt. If so, you are not loving God when you are disobeying Him, no matter how powerful your emotional experience in church.

The first commandment is to love God completely.

The other obvious error is that you attend worship services and feel nothing. But when you leave, you do your best to be obedient to everything you understand God to be asking of you. Don't assume you don't love God because you weren t moved by the music. That is the opposite error.

If you love God, you will keep His commandments, and His commandments are not burdensome (1 John 5:3). They are the pathway to joy.

4. What Did Jesus Teach Was the Second Greatest Commandment?

The second commandment is to love our neighbors as ourselves.

Jesus taught that we should love other people: "The second is like it, 'you shall love your neighbor as yourself.' On these two commandments hang all the Law and the Prophets" (Matthew 22:39–40). So, again, we come to the question, if the second greatest commandment is to love our neighbor as ourselves, what does it mean to love our neighbor? In fact, that very question was asked Jesus. During a discussion, a certain lawyer stood up and put Him to the test, saying, "Teacher, what shall I do to inherit eternal life?" And Jesus replied, "What is written in the Law? What is your reading of it?" And the lawyer answered, "You shall love the LORD your God with all your heart, with all your soul, with all your strength, and with all your mind. And your neighbor as yourself." And Jesus said to him, "You have answered rightly; do this, and you will live."

But the lawyer wanted an excuse not to be too inconvenienced by such a command. So, wanting to justify himself, he said to Jesus, "And who is my neighbor?" (Luke 10:25–29) At this point, Jesus told the parable of the Good Samaritan, a story so relevant and timeless in its truth that it is still well known even among those who do not seriously follow Scripture. In fact, you can join a Good Samaritan travel club. You put a Good Sam sticker in the window of your recreational vehicle, and if you ever have any road trouble, another Good Sam member will always stop to help you.

The story as recorded in Luke 10: 30–35 goes like this:

> A certain man was going down from Jerusalem to Jericho; and he fell among robbers, and they stripped him and beat him, and went off leaving him half dead. And by chance a certain priest was going down on that road, and when he saw him, he passed by on the other side. And likewise a Levite also, when he came to the place and saw him, passed by on the other side. But a certain Samaritan, who was on a journey, came upon him; and when he saw him, he felt compassion, and came to him, and bandaged up his wounds, pouring oil and wine on them; and he put him on his own beast, and brought him to an inn, and took care of him. And on the next day he took out two denarii and gave them to the innkeeper and said, "Take care of him; and whatever more you spend, when I return, I will repay you" (NASB).

Then Jesus asked the lawyer a question. "Which of these three do you think was a neighbor to him who fell into the thieves?" And the lawyer said, "He who showed mercy on him." Then Jesus said to him, "Go and do likewise."

What is the second greatest command? Love your neighbor as yourself. Who is your neighbor? Anyone in trouble who comes across your path whom you can help.

Let's look at each of those qualifications, because the reality is, you cannot help everyone. You don't have enough money to advertise that anyone in the whole world can go to any hospital and get all the medical attention he needs. Because you will pay for it. Besides, many people find themselves in trouble because of their own irresponsibility, and if you help them out, you are only funding their irresponsibility. Let's say a young person has been arrested for drunk driving and mischievous destruction of property. His case history shows that he feels no remorse for his actions. If you help him out by paying his bail, and paying for the damaged property, he will only go out the next night and do it again. In such a case, you are not helping him by paying for the bail and damage. You are abetting and perpetuating his irresponsibility.

We are to help those persons for whom it would be best if they were helped. Second, it must be someone who comes across your path. Third, you have to be able to meet the need. There are times when someone else has a need but you have a greater one. Let's say you have four children, and your wife has just come home from the hospital with a fifth newborn. She has not regained her strength and she has her hands full with the baby. You have your hands full with feeding, bathing, and dressing the other four children, as well as cleaning up after meals and keeping the house in order. Complications in the delivery caused medical bills that are not covered by insurance. This would not be the time to invite a visiting handbell choir from Germany to stay in your home for a week, even if they really needed some place to stay. It is time to trust God to raise up another Christian in your church to help them.

The second commandment is to love our neighbors as we love ourselves.

But, having given sufficient attention to reasonable limitations to the principles of the parable, the point of the parable remains clear. The self-righteous priest and the Levite could easily have helped, but didn't. Shame on them. And shame on us if we do not have the heart of the Samaritan, even if we cannot always help. We can at least pray for the Lord to send along someone else to help. That attitude maintains the spirit of the Good Samaritan. But let nothing hinder you from carrying out the deeds of the Good Samaritan when it is right for you to do so. That is how you fulfill the second great command. You love your neighbor as yourself. Loving God does not depend on the presence of emotional tidal waves, and neither does loving your neighbor. You do good to others when it is right to do so and when it is within your power to do so.

One of the most powerful sentences ever uttered is, "And just as you want men to do to you, you also do to them likewise" (Luke 6:31). That is the spirit of the Good Samaritan. What would you like for others to do for you if you were in their predicament?

Conclusion

Michael Green, in his superlative volume *Who Is This Jesus?* wrote:

It is not religious ritual, however worthy, that brings you into the kingdom of God but a lovely filial (son or daughter) relationship with Him. God does not want endless servants: He wants sons and daughters. It is not a question of doing lots of things for God: it is a question of allowing Him to become your loving heavenly Father and being true to that relationship. It will enevitably lead to a life of love to God and to your fellows. It is hardly surprising, in the light of all this, that the Christian word for "love," *agape*, (uh-gop´-ay) was practically introduced into the language by Jesus. It did exist beforehand—just. But until He came, nobody had seen what it really meant. Yet, if God so *loved* the world that He gave His only Son for us, why, that shed an entirely new light on love. It meant total self-giving for the totally unworthy. That is what God the Father did. That is what Jesus embodied. That is what He called on His disciples to do (36).

I chose the passage in Matthew 22:37–40 in which Jesus says that the two greatest commandments are to love God and love your fellow man because Jesus said the whole Law and the Prophets depend on these two commandments (Matthew 22:40). He was saying that the teaching of the Law and the Prophets in the Old Testament merely give detailed and specific instruction and commands on what it means to love God and love your fellow man. I think the same is true of the New Testament. If we hold to these values in our heart, we will automatically go a long way toward fulfilling all that Jesus taught.

Speed Bump!

Slow down to make sure you've gotten the main points of this chapter.

Question **A**nswer

Q1. What did Jesus teach about humanity's greatest need?

A1. Jesus taught that humanity is spiritually *lost* and needs to be saved.

Q2. What did Jesus teach about true righteousness?

A2. Jesus taught that true righteousness is *internal*, not external.

Q3. What did Jesus teach is the most important commandment?

A3. Jesus taught that we should *love* God with all our heart and soul and mind.

Fill In the Blank

Question **A**nswer

Q1. What did Jesus teach about humanity's greatest need?

A1. Jesus taught that humanity is spiritually _____ and needs to be saved.

Q2. What did Jesus teach about true righteousness?

A2. Jesus taught that true righteousness is _____, not external.

Q3. What did Jesus teach is the most important commandment?

A3. Jesus taught that we should _____ God with all our heart and soul and mind.

For Further Thought and Discussion

1. Both John the Baptist and Jesus rebuked the Pharisees for their hypocrisy of eternal religious "show" pasted over the top of greed, jealousy, and pride. Who do you think in the religious world are the counterparts of the Pharisees today?

2. Each of us is guilty to lesser and greater degrees of keeping up the show on the outside while something is not right on the inside. Is this always wrong? Can you think of examples where it might not be

wrong? Is this different than what Jesus and John condemned the Pharisees for?

3. How would you describe a person who was internally righteous? What external religious activity might he engage in and what might he excuse himself from? For example, can you be an internally righteous person and not go to church? What about reading one's Bible, praying, etc. What about negatives? How does true internal righteousness affect such historically debatable activities as going to movies, watching television, listening to rock and roll music, etc.?

What If I Don't Believe?

1. If I don't believe that humanity's greatest problem is that each person is lost and needs to be saved, I may rub shoulders with religion without ever becoming a true Christian.

2. If I don't believe that true religion is internal and not external, I may allow myself to be deceived into thinking that I am all right with God if I just go to church and do a few other things "for" Him.

3. If I don't believe that loving God means obeying Him, I may allow myself to be deceived into thinking that it doesn t matter how I live as long as I "feel in my heart" that I am okay with God.

4. If I don't believe that part of true religion is loving my neighbor as myself, I may deceive myself into thinking that I am a good Christian even though I treat other people in an un-Christian way.

For Further Study

1. Scripture
Several key passages speak to the subjects which Jesus taught. They include:

- Ephesians 2:1–10
- Matthew 22:37–40
- John 14:23–24
- John 15:10–12
- Luke 10:25–37

If you wish further study, read these passages and consider how they contribute to our understanding of what Jesus taught.

2. Books

Several other books are very helpful in studying this subject. They are listed below in general order of difficulty. If I could only read one of these, I would read the first one.

Who Is This Jesus? Michael Green
More Than a Carpenter, Josh McDowell
The Master, John Pollock
The Words and Works of Jesus Christ, J. Dwight Pentecost

If you wish to be disappointed, look to others.
If you wish to be downhearted, look to
yourself. If you wish to be encouraged . . .
look to Jesus.
■ Eric Sauer

What Did Jesus Do?

Winston Churchill, the often abrupt and caustic prime minister of England during World War II, had a very gruff exterior. His capacity to insult was legendary. Shortly before World War II Nancy Astor, the American-born wife of Waldorf, viscount Astor, visited Blenheim Palace, the ancestral home of the Churchill family. In conversation with Churchill, she expounded on the subject of women's rights, an issue that was to take her into the House of Commons as the first woman member of Parliament. Churchill opposed her on this and other causes that she held dear. In some exasperation Lady Astor said, "Winston, if I were married to you, I'd put poison in your coffee." Churchill responded, "And if you were my wife, I'd drink it."

Yet, inside this gruff exterior beat a heart that could be very tender. In the summer of 1941, Sergeant James Allen Ward was awarded the Victoria Cross for climbing out onto the wing of his Wellington bomber at 13,000 feet above the ground to extinguish a fire in the starboard engine. Secured only by a rope around his waist, he managed to smother the fire and return along the wing to the aircraft's cabin. Churchill, an admirer as well as a performer of swashbuckling exploits, summoned the shy New Zealander to 10 Downing Street. Ward, struck dumb with awe in Churchill's presence, was unable to answer the prime minister's questions. Churchill surveyed the unhappy hero with some compassion.

"You must feel very humble and awkward in my presence," he said,

"Yes, Sir," managed Ward.

"Then you can imagine how humble and awkward I feel in yours," returned Churchill.

This second story portrays Churchill somewhat differently from the first one. A person may seem crusty on the outside, yet do kind and generous deeds. So we learn to discount his gruff exterior and heed his actions. "He seems like a tough old bird, but, really, he has a soft heart," we say.

"What you do speaks so loudly I cannot hear what you say!" goes the American proverb. Another states, "Actions speak louder than words." No matter what a person says, what he *does* always wins out. That is, if a person is all sweetness and cream in his words, but his actions are self-serving and vindictive, we learn to discount what he says, and heed only what he does. "He'll say whatever you want to hear when he's speaking to your face, but turn your back, and he'll stick a verbal dagger in it," we say.

Nevertheless, we expect consistency between what a person says and what he does. We look both at what a person says and what he does to get a picture of what the person is really like. Even if a person is inconsistent, we will eventually learn what the person is really like. A person cannot hide his true self, because it is not merely a matter of what he says and does, but also what he does not say and does not do. Who we are *will* come out.

In this chapter, we learn that . . .

1. Jesus performed miracles to validate the new message of salvation He was bringing to humanity.

2. Jesus confronted the religious establishment to reveal the barrenness of their spirituality and to open access to God for the multitudes.

3. Jesus prepared for His departure by equipping a core of disciples to carry on His work in His absence.

So it is with God. If God came to earth, we would expect Him to say pretty amazing things. God *did* come to earth, and we spent the last chapter looking at what He said, and they were pretty amazing. Now, the question is, if God's words and His actions were going to be consistent, what would His actions be? What Jesus said was so astonishing, what He promised so enticing, what He claimed so magnificent that it simply will not do unless He followed such claims with equally amazing deeds. What good is it for Jesus to offer to forgive sins or bring in the kingdom of God or prepare a home for us in heaven if He were not able to fulfill His words?

Why Did Jesus Perform Miracles?

Jesus performed miracles to validate the new message of salvation He was bringing to humanity.

Many people choke at the idea of Jesus' performing of miracles. They balk at the records of miracles by both Jesus and God and go to elaborate lengths to explain them away. But what is the problem with God's doing a miracle now and then? In fact, what good is a God who can't do a miracle?

One hundred billion stars form our Milky Way Galaxy. It is difficult to get an idea how great that number is. Let's say you were up on a mountain in Colorado, looking down on a very large meadow. There would be (approximately, of course) 100 billion blades of grass in the meadow. That is how many stars there are in just our one galaxy. Now, there are 100 billion *galaxies*, some with *more* than 100 billion stars in them. And, we say 100 billion because our present telescopes can see no farther. Scientists suspect that many more exist, perhaps an endless number, filling endless space. Now God hung those stars there. That being the case, why would it be so hard for Him to perform other miracles?

According to various polls an overwhelming number of people in the United States believe in God and believe that Jesus is God. Why do people who believe in God and Jesus balk at miracles? Miracles are part of being God. If our God could not perform miracles, we would all be in big trouble, because the problems which mankind has are so great it's going to take a miracle to get us out of them.

Jesus performed miracles. We state it clearly, unapologetically, unself-consciously. He did them to meet the needs of mankind and to be consistent with the amazing things He said. He had to perform miracles in order to meet the qualifications of being God. In a very early document dated A.D. 124, only around thirty years after the death of the apostle John, a believer named Quadratus wrote to Hadrian, the Roman Emperor at the time, to encourage him to consider the truth of Christianity:

But the works of our Savior were always present (for they were genuine): namely those who were healed, those who rose from the dead. They were not only seen in the act of being healed or raised, but they remained always present. And not merely when the

Savior was on earth, but after his departure as well. They lived on for a considerable time, so much so that some of them have survived to our own day (Green, 46).

That Quadratus should write to so lofty a figure as the emperor of Rome and without hesitation claim that Jesus did miracles attests to the truth of them. Justin Martyr, an early Christian writer in his book, *Apology* (A.D. 150), wrote with confidence, "that he performed these miracles you may easily satisfy yourself from the *Acts of Pontius Pilate*." Even the Jewish leaders were not able to deny the reality of the miracles: They were too well known. Since they could not deny them, they simply attributed them to the devil ("He casts out demons by the power of Satan," they charged). To the person who assessed the evidence with an open mind, the conclusion was inescapable. Jesus performed miracles, not in isolated incidents, but on such a widespread basis that knowledge of it spread throughout that whole part of the world.

Jesus did not perform miracles merely to bedazzle or entertain, but to help people believe what He was saying. For example, he claimed to be able to forgive sins (Mark 2:5–12). **Jesus used miracles to validate his message.** Well, how do we know if He can? Anyone can say, "Your sins are forgiven you." The question is, "Are they really? How do I know?" Knowing this, Jesus followed up His announcement of forgiveness with a miracle. A man paralyzed from birth got up and walked at His command. Now that gets your attention! And Jesus said that the reason He healed the paralytic was so that people would believe that He had the power to forgive sins.

In another example (Luke 7:11–17), Jesus brought back to life a young man from the city of Nain. Many people witnessed the miracle, and "fear gripped them all", and they began glorifying God, saying, "A great prophet has arisen among us!" and "God has visited His people!" And this report concerning Him spread all over Judea, and quickly radiated to all the surrounding district.

As the report of these dramatic miracles reached the ears of John the Baptist, he sent some of his disciples to ask Jesus if He were the Messiah or if was there another to come (Luke 7:18–23). Jesus answered John's disciples, "Go and report to John what you have seen and heard: the blind receive sight, the lame walk, the lepers are cleansed, and the deaf hear, the dead are raised up, the poor have the gospel preached to them" (Luke 7:22 NASB).

Jesus here quotes from Isaiah's glorious prophecy from hundreds of years earlier (Isaiah 35:4–6). The prophet had seen in advance the time when God would come and save His people and

---

Why I need to know this

Much of Jesus' life will remain a mystery if I don't understand what He did and why He did it. For example, if I don't understand the purpose of His miracles, I won't know why He didn't heal all the people in Jerusalem, when He could have. He may seem to lack compassion for those He did not heal. I might not understand that a purpose underlay His habit of healing on the Sabbath. I need to know what Jesus did and why He did it, or many of His acts will be shrouded in mystery. He will remain a puzzle to me. I will not have as much personal trust in Him, as much appreciation for Him, or as much confidence in sharing Him with others as I could have.

---

the signs that would accompany the arrival of that salvation. Jesus in Luke 7 is telling John the Baptist that those very signs, those divine "rescue operations" Isaiah had listed, are now happening through His own ministry. John, at this time in Herod's prison and discouraged, can believe that Jesus is God's Messiah and that the long-awaited "day of salvation" has arrived in Jesus. God's great rescue is happening through the One whose name *Jesus* means "God to the rescue." And Jesus' miracles both announced this rescue and helped to perform it.

Categories of Miracles

The miracles Jesus performed fell into several categories. He healed people of physical diseases and infirmities, such as paralysis and deformed limbs. As the Great Physician, He demonstrated His power over sickness and disease. He also cast demons out of people. Many used to scoff at this until the last twenty years in which we have seen a dramatic rise in Satan worship, witchcraft, and demonic activity. The knowledgeable no longer scoff. Jesus cast demons out of little boys, out of social outcasts, out of everyday people. This showed His power over the forces of darkness.

Jesus stilled storms. More than once, He was on the Sea of

Galilee when a terrible storm hit, threatening to sink the boat. At His rebuke, the wind calmed and the waves smoothed out. This revealed His power over nature. And all was intended to give people a reason to believe that He was who He said He was. He claimed to be the light of the world, and He healed a blind man. He claimed to be the bread of life, and He fed the five thousand with two loaves and five fish. He claimed to be the resurrection and the life, and He brought back Lazarus from the dead. The link between His words and His deeds is inescapable. He intended it to be.

At the end of His life, Jesus was in an upper room with His disciples, sharing a time of worship, fellowship, and final instruction before His crucifixion. We read of this in the Gospel of John, chapter 13–17. In John 17:4, Jesus says, "I have glorified You on the earth, I have finished the work which You have given Me to do." Well, how in the world could Jesus say He had accomplished the work He had to do? Look at all the sick people still in the area. Look at all the demon-possessed people. Look at all the injured and suffering. If you have ever suffered deeply, you understand why the Gospels talk about these enormous crowds crushing down upon Him for a chance to be healed. Suffering was epidemic. Multitudes would have done anything to have a chance to be freed from it.

Jesus had hardly scratched the surface of suffering in that part of the world, let alone the rest of the world. How then could Jesus, with His having the capacity to heal all that hurt and pain, say that He had accomplished the work He had to do?

The Purposes of Jesus' Miracles

The answer is that He did not come to earth to alleviate all human suffering during His time on earth. As God, He could easily have done that from heaven with one snap of His divine finger. But He came to earth to carry out God's great rescue of humanity in a different way, and His miracles helped carry out that rescue in several ways. First, they obviously did rescue people from various kinds of suffering and predicaments. Second, in those acts of rescue, the miracles demonstrated the truth about who God is and what He is like: He is the God who saves, who cares about all human suffering and predicaments, and who not only cares, but who is also powerful enough to snatch people from the jaws of their torment. While Jesus did not relieve all human suffering in the world, it is clear that He was touched by the suffering He encountered and did not heal or perform other miracles only to make a theological point. He really cared about people and their pain.

Third, some miracles showed that a major part of the human predicament is bondage to real and supernatural evil. People really were tormented in bondage to the devil and his cohorts, and the miracle of casting out demons demonstrated that God is completely powerful over the devil. That miracle also showed that the devil's control over humans is now broken, through Jesus. Fourth, the miracles of raising people from the dead showed the ultimate destruction of death itself. Especially in this kind of miracle, we can see how the miracles aimed to help people see who Jesus really is and to believe in Him and in the message of salvation He proclaimed.

The miracles don't and can't force anyone to believe. But they fulfill perhaps their chief purpose when they *challenge* those who received them and those who witnessed them (including we who witness them today through reading about them). They challenged those of Jesus' time and they challenge us to believe in Jesus as God's great Rescuer, as our Savior, as the One through whom our sins are forgiven, our fellowship with God and one another is restored, and our freedom from the nasty power of all manner of evil is ultimately guaranteed. The miracles challenge us to believe Jesus' message that, apart from God's forgiveness, we are dead in our sins and that His death on the cross provides that forgiveness to us who believe.

In Hebrews 2:3–4, we see this principle stated clearly. The writer of the book of Hebrews asks,

> How shall we escape if we neglect so great a salvation? After it [this new message of salvation] was at the first spoken through the Lord [Jesus], it was confirmed to us by those who heard, God also bearing witness with them [the people who had the new message confirmed], both by signs and wonders and by various miracles and by gifts of the Holy Spirit according to His own will.

Yes, Jesus' words were amazing, and for Him to be consistent, His deeds had to be amazing, too. As we read the New Testament, He does not disappoint us.

Why Did Jesus Confront the Religious Establishment?

Jesus confronted the religious establishment to reveal the barrenness of their spirituality and to open access to God for the multitudes.

Three groups of people in the religious establishment are commonly referred to in the New Testament: scribes, Pharisees and Sadducees (Matthew 23:13, Matthew 3:7). Despite their differences all of them had drifted from true spiritual commitment to God and to His Law, and were hung up on self-gratification and self-exaltation. They used the Law as their means of climbing the ladder of social power, not of leading people to genuine relationships with God.

It is easy to miss the true motivation of the religious leaders. Though some of them accepted Jesus, the ones who maintained the stronghold in Jerusalem eventually became so jealous of their turf and Jesus' popularity that they demanded Jesus be killed, even though no true charges could be brought against Him. Jesus clearly objected to this cold-hearted group in Matthew 23 because . . .

- Their teachings keep men from entering the kingdom of heven, because instead of a heart commitment to God, they teach a rigid adherence to traditions. This, perhaps, is the greatest sin of all.
- They devoured "widows' houses" by exploiting their usually meager resources.
- As master hypocrites, they put on a big show of public piety, to impress others with their religious correctness.
- They went to great efforts to make a new convert, but when they did, the new convert became twice as bad as they were.
- They fulfilled the little parts of the law, like tithing herbs, but in big things like taking care of their needy parents (acts of love and mercy to humans), they violated the law.
- They held themselves up to the public as very righteous people, but in their hearts, they were robbers and gluttons.
- They paid tribute to prophets of old by building monuments to them, but killed the modern ones.

When you look at this stark list of indictments against these religious leaders, it is no wonder that John the Baptist and Jesus took them on so forcefully. Dangerous enemies of the gospel, they were responsible for teaching things which, if believed, would keep a person from being saved. And they did it because they were selfish, jealous, money-grubbing and power-hungry.

By exposing false spirituality, Jesus stimulated conflict.
Because of the gigantic obstacle these people presented to the gospel, Jesus had no choice but to challenge them, and in so doing, He revealed their hypocrisy. He initiated Sabbath controversies by deliberately doing things on the Sabbath which were proper in God's sight, but which the religious leaders objected to. Second, He was friendly toward "sinners" whom the religious leaders looked down upon as hopelessly unholy. Third, He purposely challenged those traditions that distorted God's intentions and thus blocked people's access to God. Jesus demonstrated that these traditions were not part of the Mosaic Law. He did these things as the Savior, hoping to move these leaders to change by revealing their hypocrisy, and declaring "the year of God's favor" to the multitudes harmed by evil leadership. Let's look at each of these a little more closely.

1. Jesus Initiated Sabbath Controversies

In order not to break the Sabbath, the Pharisees made up and kept traditions stricter even than the Sabbath Laws of Moses. That way, if they slipped up, they might break a tradition, but not a law. A modern analogy might be that if the law says you can only drive 55 miles per hour, the Jewish tradition would allow you to drive only 45 miles per hour. Then, if you were not paying sufficient attention and you inadvertently went 50 miles an hour, you would have broken a tradition, but not a law.

Jesus kept the Law, as we read in Matthew 5:17: "Do not think that I came to destroy the Law or the Prophets. I did not come to destroy but to fulfill." But He shattered harmful traditions raised up around the Law. And the Jewish leaders, attached to these traditions, went after him with fangs bared. The Pharisees allowed very little that was not essential to go on during the Sabbath. When Jesus healed people on the Sabbath, which He did on at least six occasions, it caused a truly alarming level of anger from the Pharisees. After one such healing, they made up their mind to kill Him.

Jesus walked through grainfields on the Sabbath, and His disciples became hungry and began to pick the heads of grain and eat. This incensed the Pharisees. Jesus made it clear, however, that the disciples had not violated the Sabbath. From that altercation, He went directly to their synagogue. A man with a withered hand was there. The Pharisees asked Jesus if it were lawful to heal on the Sabbath. They wanted an excuse to accuse Him. Jesus asked, "What man is there among you who has one sheep, and if it falls into a pit on the Sabbath, will not lay hold of it and lift it out? Of how much more value then is a man than a sheep? Therefore, it is lawful to do good on the Sabbath." Then He promptly healed the man. With equal promptness, the Pharisees went out and had a committee meeting to decide how to kill Him (Matthew 12:1–14).

This pattern is repeated many times in the Gospels. Jesus healed a woman who had been doubled over for eighteen years with a sickness caused by a spirit (Luke 13:10–17), a man with dropsy (Luke 14:1–5), an infirm man at the Pool of Bethesda who had been sick for thirty-eight years (John 5:1–10), and a man born blind (John 9:1–34). Every incident caused an uproar. Clearly, Jesus was meeting the hypocrites head on. He wanted to expose the bankruptcy and selfishness of the Pharisaical traditions. He did it. The crowds' ecstasy only fueled the Pharisees hatred. Jesus made it very clear that true righteousness is internal, not external. Each time He healed a person on the Sabbath, He verified the whole point of the Sermon on the Mount, and the Pharisees hated Him for it. It exposed the barrenness of their hearts. It takes a cold heart not to be happy about a miraculous healing, no matter the day of the week.

2. Jesus Welcomed Contact with Sinners

The Pharisees prided themselves in the fact that they never came in contact with sinners: They viewed it as evidence of their purity. Jesus, however, readily associated with sinners. This was a direct affront to religious leaders, and, by implication, exposed the bleakness of their lives. Many times in the Gospels we read about the religious leaders' grumbling because Jesus ate with tax gatherers and sinners.

Tax gatherers were Jews who accepted from the Romans the job of collecting Jewish taxes for Rome. In the process, they often lined their own pockets as well. Other Jews were viewed as the scum of the earth because they aided and abetted the Roman domination of the Jews, and did it for money. Matthew 9 gives a typical example. Jesus and His disciples were eating with a group of tax gatherers and sinners. The Pharisees said, "Why does your Teacher eat with tax gatherers and sinners?" When Jesus learned what was being discussed, He gave His standard answer: "Those who are well have no need of a physician, but those who are sick" (verse 12).

Three kinds of religious leaders in the New Testament:

1. *Scribes:* profound scholars of the Law. Their knowledge of the Old Testament Law was at times astonishing. They also taught the Law and were often called upon to clarify religious disputes.

2. *Pharisees:* religious rigorists who believed in a life of sharp separation from Gentiles and strict adherence to the Mosaic Law. Their traditions were even stricter than the Law, so that by keeping their traditions they would be unlikely ever to break the Law. However, Jesus accused them of breaking the Law in order to keep their traditions.

3. *Sadducees:* religious aristocrats who considered it prudent to get along with the Gentiles, to "live and let live." Less rigorous theologically, they were often very wealthy because they had more liberal scruples about their dealings with Gentiles.

In another account, Zaccheus, a different tax collector, went out of his way to meet Jesus (Luke 19:4). Seeing faith and repentance growing in the man's heart, Jesus invited Himself to Zaccheus's house for dinner that night. Again, the Pharisees complained that Jesus had gone to be the guest of a sinner.

From the point of view of the Pharisees, Luke 7 records the most outrageous incident. Jesus was dining in the home of a Pharisee (a very respectable thing to do) when a prostitute came into the house and began anointing Jesus' feet with costly oil. Her tears of repentance dripped onto Jesus' feet, and she wiped them off with her long hair. This revolted the Pharisees. If Jesus were a true prophet, they reasoned, He would know what sort of woman was doing this awkward and untimely thing. Jesus' response vindicated her actions as being a sign of her repentance.

3. Jesus Deliberately Challenged the Pharisees

The Jews had many traditions, which they raised to a level of importance equal to the Law, and it became as serious in their minds to break such a tradition as a law. They faithfully observed these traditions. However, they would sometimes violate a law in order to observe a tradition. One day, Jesus and His disciples were walking through a field of grain and being hungry, they began to eat some of it. The Pharisees saw this and asked Jesus why His disciples violated the Sabbath. Jesus, of course, defended His disciples' actions.

In a more blatant exchange in Mark 7, we read a clear account of the issues:

And the Pharisees and some of the scribes gathered together around Him when they had come from Jerusalem, and had seen that some of His disciples were eating their bread with impure hands, that is, unwashed. (For the Pharisees and all the Jews do not eat unless they carefully wash their hands, thus observing the traditions of the elders; and when they come from the market place, they do not eat unless they cleanse themselves; and there are many other things which they have received in order to observe, such as the washing of cups and pitchers and copper pots.)

And the Pharisees and the scribes asked Him, "Why do Your disciples not walk according to the tradition of the elders, but eat their bread with impure hands?" And He said to them, "Rightly did Isaiah prophesy of you hypocrites, as it is written, 'this people honors Me with their lips, but their heart is far away from Me. But in vain do they worship Me, teaching as doctrines the precepts of men.' Neglecting the commandment of God, you hold to the tradition of men."

He was also saying to them, "You nicely set aside the commandment of God in order to keep your tradition. For Moses said, 'Honor your father and your mother'; and, 'He who speaks evil of father or mother, let him be put to death'; but you say, 'If a man says to his father or his mother, anything of mine you might have been helped by is Corban (that is to say, given to God),' you no longer permit him to do anything for his father or his mother; thus invalidating the word of God by your tradition which you have handed down; and you do many things such as that" (Mark 7:1–13 NASB).

In these ways, then, Jesus confronted the religious establishment, to reveal the infertility of the Pharisee's traditions, and to call people to a true relationship with God.

How Did Jesus Prepare for His Departure?

Jesus prepared for His departure by equipping a core of disciples to carry on in His absence.

Almost from the moment He began His ministry, Jesus began preparing for His departure. He was well aware of the fact that He would be crucified at the hands of evil and unscrupulous men. His great concern in this, of course, was that the message of salvation would be well established in the minds of the multitudes, and that He would have a core of disciples prepared to spread the message after He left them. Therefore, we see in the Gospels this two-fold approach to establishing His message. Jesus would at times speak to great multitudes of people. In the well-known miracle of feeding the five thousand with just two loaves of bread and five fish, the five thousand were men only. If they had their wives and children with them, there may have been as many as ten thousand or more. Many of the crowds He spoke to were enormous, and his public ministry resulted in His being known throughout that region of the world.

Jesus equipped His followers to broadcast His message. In addition, He often withdrew from public ministry, and spent time just with His disciples. He had an outer group of followers which numbered in the hundreds or perhaps thousands. He had a team of seventy more involved people. Finally, He had his twelve disciples who were with Him all the time. Within the twelve, He was especially close to Peter, James and John. Into these people on a life-on-life basis, He was forming the nucleus of a following which would take the message of salvation to the world after He was crucified.

This, then, is what Jesus spent the bulk of His time doing during His brief three-year ministry: First, He performed miracles, not only out of compassion to relieve human suffering, but to verify that He was the Messiah, and to validate the message of salvation He was preaching. Second, He confronted the religious leaders in an attempt to reveal the falseness of their religion, and to call people to a true relationship with the living God. Third, He prepared for His departure by spreading the message of salvation to the multitudes and by readying a team of disciples equipped to carry the message of salvation to the world after He was crucified.

Speed Bump!

Slow down long enough to be sure you've gotten the main points of this chapter.

Question   **Q1.** Why did Jesus perform miracles?

Answer   **A1.** To validate the new *message* of salvation He was bringing to humanity.

Q2. Why did Jesus confront the religious establishment?

A2. To reveal the *barrenness* of their spirituality and to open *access* to God for the multitudes.

Q3. How did Jesus prepare for His departure?

A3. By equipping a core of *disciples* to carry on His work in His absence.

Fill In the Blank

Question   **Q1.** Why did Jesus perform miracles?

Answer   **A1.** To validate the new _____ He was bringing to humanity.

Q2. Why did Jesus confront the religious establishment?

A2. To reveal the _____ of their spirituality and to open _____ to God for the multitudes.

Q3. How did Jesus prepare for His departure?

A3. By equipping a core of _____ to carry on His work in His absence.

For Further Thought and Discussion

1. Why do you think Jesus did not heal everyone in Jerusalem before He left? Is that not really asking the same question as Why does God allow pain in the world? What do you think?

2. Do you see any conflict between Jesus' admonition to us to "turn the other cheek" and His strong denunciation of the Pharisees? How do you resolve the two?

3. Does it seem risky to you that Jesus left His entire spiritual kingdom on earth in the hands of a few people who were pretty shaky in their understanding and confidence when He was crucified?

What If I Don't Believe?

1. If I don't believe that Jesus performed miracles in order to validate the new message of salvation He was bringing, I might not understand why He performed some miracles and not others. His miracles seem random and not always in keeping with the needs of the people to whom He was ministering. For example, why would He turn water into wine at a wedding party, but not heal all the paralytics in the city? The reason is that His purpose was not to relieve all human suffering, but to help people believe in both who He was, and the new message He was bringing.

2. If I don't believe that Jesus confronted the religious establishment to reveal their spiritual bankruptcy, I might just think He was being hard to get along with, and picking fights with people. Rather, He timed His controversies with them to disclose their spiritual sterility in order to encourage them to repent, and to embolden their followers to reject their leadership.

3. If I don't believe that Jesus intended to leave His spiritual kingdom in the hands of His few followers, I might think that He lost control of events at the end, and was crucified prematurely. However, He planned all along to reach the world through His followers, one convert at a time. He also knew that He would be sending the Holy Spirit to indwell all His followers, and to guide and energize the spread of the message of salvation through Christ to the ends of the earth for all time.

For Further Study

1. Scripture
Several key passages in the Bible speak of what Jesus did on earth and why. They include:

- Hebrews 2:3–4
- 1 Peter 1:21–24
- Matthew 28:18–20

If you wish further study, read these passages and consider how they contribute to your understanding of what Jesus did and why. Actually, all of the New Testament witnesses to what Jesus did. The Gospels relate this activity directly in stories, narrative. The remaining books of the New Testament express the meanings of Jesus' earthly activity and His ongoing activity through His followers, who make up the Church.

2. Books

Several other books are very helpful in studying further this subject. They are listed below in general order of difficulty. If I could read only one of these, I would read the first one.

Who Is This Jesus? Michael Green
More Than a Carpenter, Josh McDowell
The Master, John Pollock
The Words and Works of Jesus Christ, J. Dwight Pentecost

A Savior who is not quite God is like a bridge broken at the further end.
■ **Bishop Moule**

5

What Did Jesus Accomplish on Earth?

Tolstoy's towering novel, *War and Peace*, tells of the invasion of Russia by Napoleon in 1812. Petya, the young son of a rich and powerful Russian family, is too young to serve in the military, but old enough to want to. He watches in undisguised admiration as the Russian armies march out to war against the European invaders. He longs to go with them. He hounds his father, without success, to let him join. As Napoleon and the French army press down upon the city of Moscow, it is clear after several resounding defeats that the Russian army cannot prevent the invasion of their glorious mother city. In a wildly unexpected but strategically ingenious move, the commander of the Russian army orders the total evacuation of the entire city of Moscow, both civilian as well as military. He also orders the city to be set on fire so that Napoleon would not find a comfortable retreat in the city. It was an unthinkable maneuver, but the secret to the ultimate Russian victory.

Napoleon was stunned and deeply offended that there was no military delegation in Moscow to surrender to him. Not only that, he was absolutely stymied. He did not know what to do. He knew it was useless to pursue the fleeing citizens and an elusive army capable of outmaneuvering him as they fled to the wilderness. Also, it was fruitless to wait in Moscow, because no one was there to surrender, and no one to provide food and water for his 200,000 soldiers. With winter coming on, he could only retreat to France in utter humiliation. He had invaded Russia, had gone right to her very heart, but was not able to conquer her. As they retreated, the French suffered terrible losses. Cold, lack of food, and demoralization reduced the French army to a disorganized herd of humanity, hustling to escape the jaws of the Russian winter before they snapped shut on them. As the French army fled Russia, the Russian army pursued them, inflicting, along with the weather, terrible losses. The war was over. Russia had been saved.

During the time that Napoleon was waiting in vain in Moscow for a military delegation to come and sue for peace, Petya finally told his father (no longer asking) that he was going to go join the army. Unable to stop him, his father gave him his blessing. Petya had a romantic notion that with his saber and mighty charger, he would drive the French invaders out of his mother land, and return to Moscow in triumph. The thought of anything terrible happening to him never crossed his mind.

Then, as the French army was fleeing certain disaster, its defeat already obvious to everyone, the salvation of his mother land already secured, young Petya rode in a ridiculous cavalry charge against a small contingent of French soldiers in an utterly insignificant and militarily meaningless operation. With visions of glory dancing in his head, he charged a small pocket of French soldiers, and took a bullet in his heart. He was dead before his body hit the ground.

What a tragic and meaningless end to a misguided life! His life and death accomplished nothing. How tragic it was!

Just as the fictional Petya's life was tragic and meaningless, there are those who view the life and death of Jesus of Nazareth as equally tragic and meaningless. This towering character from Nazareth spoke words men had never heard before. "Love your neighbor. . . . Love even your enemy. Do good to those who despitefully use you. When someone strikes you on one cheek, turn the other to him. Do unto others as you would have others do unto you." He put together a moral

---

In this chapter, we learn that:

1. Jesus revealed that God's love is so great that nothing can keep us from God if we will but come to Him.
2. Jesus revealed that life is to be lived in total trust in and obedience to our heavenly Father.
3. Through Jesus we are forgiven of our sins, reconciled to God, and made ready for heaven.

---

code superior to anything ever seen on earth. He tried to get others to follow him, to accept the moral code, to help bring peace on earth and goodwill toward all men. But in the end, this poor, misguided, overoptimistic young preacher from Galilee hung from a cross, dying a ghastly death for nothing. The world heard His words, spit in His face, and then killed Him. What a tragedy. What a senseless loss. How meaningless, they say.

Oh, but they are wrong. Jesus' death was not meaningless. Tragic, yes, in a sense. But not misguided. Not worthless. Not without meaning. Quite the opposite. Napoleon mistakenly equated the Russians' retreat with their defeat when instead it led to their victory. Similarly, when Jesus went to the cross, it had every earthly appearance of defeat, but it was actually the very source of victory. Jesus' death was not only not meaningless, but it also accomplished the most significant thing in the history of humankind since the creation and fall of Adam. It achieved redemption, deliverance from a hopeless destiny. It brought hope for eternal life.

We have looked at the life of Jesus. We have looked at what He taught and what He did. We have looked at His death, burial and resurrection. Now, we must ask the question, "What did Jesus accomplish?" As we consider the answer, we will look at several things.

What Did Jesus Reveal to Us About God's Love for Us?

Jesus revealed that God's love is so great that nothing can keep us from God if we will but come to Him.

In Charles Dickens' classic novel, *A Tale of Two Cities*, there are two men who look very much alike. One is a nobleman, not only in title but in character. The other is a scoundrel who is only a scoundrel because he has never found anything in life great enough to give him meaning. Both men fall in love with the same woman, the nobleman outwardly, the scoundrel inwardly. The nobleman travels to France during the French revolution when heads of the aristocracy were dropping from the guillotine's blade like ripe apples from a tree in a strong wind. In the process of trying to save innocent aristocrats, he is arrested and destined for the guillotine himself. The scoundrel begins to awaken to nobler impulses within as a result of loving the beautiful lady, who treats him with dignity and respect. Out of love for her, and out of a desire to atone for the worthlessness of his life until then, the scoundrel cunningly steals his way into the prison where the nobleman is held, sneaks him out of the prison and unbeknownst to the nobleman, takes the nobleman's place in his cell. Since they look so much alike, no one is the wiser. The nobleman is whisked back to England and reunited with his beloved. A short time later, the scoundrel, who is no longer a scoundrel, but a nobleman himself in his heart, dies in the nobleman's place. "It is a far, far greater thing I do," he said as he was about to die, "than I have ever done; it is a far, far better rest that I go to, than I have ever known." His love for the woman who had treated him with dignity and respect was so great, he was willing to die for her betrothed so that she could be happy.

How would you feel if you were the nobleman and discovered that the other man had died in your place? What wonderment, what gratitude, what awe you would feel for the one **Nothing is greater than God's love toward us.** who offered the ultimate sacrifice. That fictional example is but a pale shadow of the love that Jesus has for us, and of the magnitude of His sacrifice for us. Jesus said, "Greater love has no man than this, than to lay down one's life for his friends" (John 15:13). And Jesus' love reached beyond this, because He laid down His life for His enemies. The apostle Paul wrote,

> For while we were still helpless, at the right time Christ died for the ungodly. For one will hardly die for a righteous man; though perhaps for the good man someone would dare even to die. But God demonstrates His own love toward us, in that while we were yet sinners, Christ died for us. (Romans 5:6–8 NASB)

A contemporary writer, Michael Green, points out that

> He loved so much that He was willing to identify with His creatures in the worst agonies of suffering and death so that nobody would ever be able to point the finger at God and say, "He doesn't understand." He does understand. He has stood in our shoes. He has suffered as no one has ever suffered. He died the worst death it was possible to die. The Cross was an example of supreme love" (*Who Is This Jesus*, 69).

What Did Jesus Reveal About How To Live Life?

Jesus revealed that life is to be lived in total trust in and obedience to our heavenly Father.

Jesus came not only to die for us, but also to show us how to live. You have probably discovered that life can be very difficult, even cruel. A common, urgent question people ask is, "Why me?" when pain invades their life. You may have grown up in a difficult family where you did not feel loved or were abused. You may be or have been in a marriage like that. You may even be in a work situation in which you do not feel respected or appreciated. You may even be treated dreadfully—used and taken advantage of. You may be suffering physical pain, or bearing the pain and suffering of a loved one. You may be distressed over the hurt and hunger you see in the world.

Jesus was no stranger to all this. He was "a man of sorrows and acquainted with grief." He experienced continual rejection, misunderstanding, and opposition up until He was finally killed. Yet in all this, He was a gentleman, faithful to His heavenly Father, and steadfast in His character. The apostle Peter wrote,

> For this finds favor, if for the sake of conscience toward God a man bears up under sorrows when suffering unjustly. For what credit is there if, when you sin and are harshly treated, you endure it with patience? But if when you do what is right and suffer for it you patiently endure it, this finds favor with God. For you have been called for this purpose, since Christ also suffered for you, leaving you an example for you to follow in His steps, who committed no sin, nor was any deceit found in His mouth; and while being reviled, He did not revile in return; while suffering, He uttered no threats, but kept entrusting {Himself} to Him who judges righteously" (1 Peter 2:19–23 NASB).

We are to trust and obey God. Jesus' life of patience, compassion, and love was intended to be an example for us. In our difficult family situation, in our burdensome marriage, in our troublesome work condition, in our personal pain, or in our having to watch suffering in those we love, we are to bear it as Jesus did, continually entrusting ourselves to Him who judges righteously and will see that all is right in the end. Mother Teresa, the saintly nun who ministers to the sick and dying in Calcutta, once said that when we get to heaven, this life will be of no more consequence than a bad night in a cheap hotel. That is hard to accept when we are tossing around in the middle of the night on the lumpy mattress of life, but focusing on that truth will help us endure the pain of this life as Jesus did.

What Did Jesus' Life Accomplish for Our Eternal Destiny?

Through Jesus we are forgiven of our sins, reconciled to God, and made ready for heaven.

Forgiveness

One thing, and only one thing separates us from God: sin. Therefore, only one thing needs to be done to reconcile us to God: remove our sin. However, removing sin in the human heart is like removing a crack from window. It can't be done.

Imagine you are a window manufacturer who has received the contract to supply windows for the space shuttles. These windows withstand enormous pressure and heat on take-off and landing, and they must conform perfectly to specifications. So, you make your first window, and there is ever-so slight a crack in it. You don't want to lose the large amount of money you've put into its manufacture. Besides, your reputation as a window-maker is on the line. You rationalize. *"It's such a small crack. I'm sorry the crack is there. I didn't mean to crack it. I won't crack the next one."* And after all that brilliant rationalization, you put the window in the shuttle. Then, along comes the NASA inspector. He inspects the shuttle minutely. At first, he doesn't see the crack. But then, he scrutinizes the window, and bingo! He finds the crack. "This window must be replaced," he says.

"Oh, but you don't understand," you reply. "It's such a small crack. I'm sorry the crack is there. I didn't mean to crack it. I won't crack the next one. Please, can't we leave the window in?"

The government inspector patiently explains: "Because of the demands of the shuttle, the window must be perfect. Anything less than perfect is unacceptable. Granted it is a small crack. I believe you didn't mean to crack it. True, it only cracked once. And you very well may not crack the next window. But the window must be perfect. This one is not perfect. There is no way you can make it perfect. Once it is cracked, you cannot un-crack it. There is only one solution. You must put in a new window."

The point is obvious, but let me elaborate. **Jesus reconciled us to God.** To get into heaven, a person must be perfect. Each of us has sinned. Each of us is imperfect. Each of us is born "cracked." There is no way you can un-sin. It may be true that you are sorry about the sin. It may be that you only sinned once (I doubt it!). It may be true you will never sin again (Ha!). But that doesn't change the fact that there is at least one sin, and you cannot get into heaven with even one sin. Your sin must be forgiven, and there must be a new "you."

Regeneration

This is entirely possible, but only one way. You must be born again, this time perfect . . . uncracked, accomplished only by believing in Jesus and receiving Him as your personal savior (John 1:12). When we place our faith in Christ, our old self is mysteriously crucified with Christ. In Galatians 2:20, the apostle Paul writes, "I have been crucified with Christ; and it is no longer I who live, but Christ lives in me." In Romans 6, Paul writes our old self was crucified with Christ (verse 6), so that as Christ was raised from the dead through the glory of the Father, we too might walk in newness of life (verse 4).

Jesus said to Nicodemus in John 3, "Do not marvel that I said to you, 'You must be born again.' " (verse 7). This new "you" that is born again is perfect. Paul writes in Ephesians, "put on the new man which was created according to God, in righteousness and true holiness" (4:24). Because the old self has been crucified in Christ and born again in Christ, Paul declares that "there is therefore now no condemnation to those who are in Christ Jesus" (Romans 8:1). The window has been replaced. The old window has been removed and a new un-cracked one put in.

That is how we get to heaven. It is through the work which Jesus did, not anything that we did. The only work for us to do is to believe in Jesus. "This is the work of God, that you believe in Him whom He sent" (John 6:29). Jesus did the work. We believe and receive. God does the rest. As we saw in earlier chapters, Jesus was both God and man. Only someone who was both God and man could do what He did, and could affect what He did. If He were not man, He could not have died for the sins of humanity. If He were not God, it would not have mattered that He did.

Justification

Jesus removed sin, the one thing which separates humans from God. But Jesus accomplished many other facets of our salvation. He provided a way for us to be forgiven, yes, and to be born again. But when our sins were forgiven, we were justified, that is, declared righteous by God.

The *Evangelical Dictionary of Theology* defines justification as "to pronounce, accept, and treat as [righteous], and not . . . liable, and, on the other hand, entitled to all the privileges due to those who have kept the laws" (593). It means more than that the charge of sin against us has been dropped. It is as though the charge was never made. It makes a person, as has been commonly said, "just as if I'd never sinned." Yet there is still more, because in justifying us, God actually credits the righteousness achieved by Jesus Christ to us. More than being forgiven, more even than being declared forgiven and innocent, justification means that God clothes us in the positive righteousness of Jesus Christ, and He sees us as righteous (because of Jesus) evermore.

While this seems to be, initially, a wonderful thing, a second thought makes us ask, "How can God see us as righteous, as though we had never sinned, when we ourselves know we have sinned? And we have sinned after our reconciliation with God. Why doesn't further sin cause a need for reconciliation again?"

The issue of justification has divided Christians for centuries. It was the central dividing issue between Catholics and Protestants during the Reformation, and even divides people today. The trouble often surrounds the issue of sin, and whether or how much a Christian can sin and still maintain his salvation. The flip side of that is the issue of how a righteous person can sin. Does God look the other way when we sin? Does He pretend He doesn't see? Does He not "sweat the small stuff?" Doesn't He care about white lies and blind spots? How can God declare us righteous if we sin?

In addressing this very sticky problem, we must make it clear that God does, indeed, declare us righteous. Our central passage states it in no uncertain terms: "having been justified by faith, we have peace with God through our Lord Jesus Christ" (Romans 5:1). But how are we justified? Paul states it earlier in Romans 4:2–3:

"For if Abraham was justified by works, he has something to boast about; but not before God. For what does the Scripture say? "And Abraham believed God, and it was reckoned to him as righteousness." We see, then, in this passage that justification brings about righteousness. We are justified, and all God's children have always been justified, by faith (NASB).

When we are born again, it is our spirit that is reborn. Our body is not reborn, as Nicodemus correctly observes in John 3. Our reborn spirit is born in the likeness of God, created in righteousness and holiness of the truth (Ephesians 4:24). Paul calls this

---

Why I need to know this

1. If I don't understand what Jesus accomplished for me, I miss the very meaning of Christianity itself. I miss the very mind of God and intention of Jesus coming to earth. If I don't understand that the central purpose in Jesus' coming was to deliver me from my sin, I miss the whole message of the Bible. I may be blinded into thinking that Jesus was merely a good man who lived an exemplary life which we would do well to model.

2. Because I would have completely misunderstood the intention and strategy of God, I would be useless in helping others deal with the central problem in their lives. I would have a message of goodness to share, but so do many other people. What I need is a message of deliverance, and no one can deliver humanity except Jesus.

---

the inner man in Romans 7, and refuses to attribute any sin to it (Romans 7:20). This inner man, this reborn spirit, is righteous. It is not the reborn spirit, but the flesh that sins (again, Romans 7). Paul states that we eagerly await the completion of our adoption as sons, namely the redemption of our bodies (Romans 8:23). So our redemption has two stages. In the first stage our spirit is redeemed and born again. This spirit is holy and righteous. Our body isn't yet redeemed, so it is not holy and righteous, but it is to be governed by our newborn spirits, which are themselves led by God's Holy Spirit. Therefore, in a way that exceeds our wisdom or understanding of Scripture, a civil war wages within a person between his newborn "inner man" and his yet-resisting flesh. It is as John MacArthur wrote in his commentary on Ephesians:

> Biblical terminology does not say that a Christian has two different natures. He has but one nature, the new nature in Christ. The old self dies and the new self lives; they do not coexist. . . . The Christian is a single new person, a totally new creation, not a spiritual schizophrenic. It is the filthy coat . . . in which the new creation dwells that continues to hinder and contaminate his living. He is no longer the old man corrupted, but is now the new

man created in righteousness and holiness, awaiting full salvation (Romans 13:11) when he dies and is given a new body (164).

In Romans 7, Paul refuses to attribute sin to the inner man, the spiritual new creation who is born again in Jesus. He goes out of his way to distinguish between the regenerate inner man and the flesh, and places sin at the doorstep of the flesh. This does not answer all questions, such as How or why, then, is the person held accountable for sin? But because the clear statements raise subsequent difficult questions is no reason to deny the clear statements. We are one nature, and that nature has been created in true holiness and righteousness, in the very likeness of God (Ephesians 4:24). It wishes to do good, joyfully concurs with the law of God, serves the law of God, and experiences no condemnation (Romans 7:21, 22, 25; 8:1).

Therefore, God does not slyly look the other way when we sin. Rather, He is looking at our spiritual self which has been redeemed, regenerated, and born again in righteousness. He is well aware that "if I am the doing the very thing I do not wish, I am no longer the one doing it, but sin which dwells in me" (Romans 7:20 NASB). While our total self is still held accountable for the sin (Romans 6:1) the sin itself does not come from the "inward man" (Romans 7:22). Just as the inner man had to die and be reborn before it could be made fit for heaven, so our bodies will die, and we will be given new ones, untouched and untainted by sin (Romans 8:23). God looks now at our inner man, already redeemed, looks forward to the redemption of our body, and declares us truly righteous in Christ.

What happens when we are justified? Well, as we have already seen, we have peace with God (Romans 5:1). We are saved from God's wrath through Christ (Romans 5:9). We are glorified (Romans 8:30). We become heirs, having the hope of eternal life (Titus 3:7).

Nothing *we* can do will make us righteous before God. As Paul wrote in Galatians, "a man is not justified by the works of the Law but by faith in Jesus Christ" (2:16). In Titus 3:5–7, we read,

> He saved us, not on the basis of deeds which we have done in righteousness, but according to His mercy, by the washing of regeneration and renewing by the Holy Spirit, whom He poured out upon us richly through Jesus Christ our Savior, that being justified

by His grace we might be made heirs according to the hope of eternal life (NASB).

We are justified by faith, that is, declared righteous, because we *are* righteous in Christ.

Redemption

All this accomplishes our redemption, which means "to be bought back." The late Donald Gray Barnhouse, former pastor of the venerable Tenth Presbyterian Church in Philadelphia, used to tell a story which pictured redemption. The story went something like this. A young boy received a toy sailboat for his birthday. He treasured it greatly. One day, while he was sailing it in a pond in one of the city parks, a strong rain storm came up. The high wind swept the sailboat to the other side of the pond, and the hard rain caused the overflow to be high enough to sweep the boat into the city water drainage system. The young boy was heartbroken, but there was nothing he could do. The boat was lost.

Some time later, he was walking down the street past a toy store. He stopped and looked in the window. There stood his very own sailboat in proud display. He rushed inside to claim it. "See," he told the proprietor, "it even has my initials carved into the hull." "I'm sorry, lad," the proprietor said. "Someone brought that boat in here the other day and sold it to me. The boat is now mine. It could be a pure coincidence that the initials on the boat are the same as yours. You can have the boat, but you ll have to pay me what I paid for it."

Well, the youngster did not have the purchase price, so went home even more dejected than before. The boat was his, but he couldn't possess it. It was not fair.

That evening when his father returned home from work, the boy poured out his story. The next day, the father went down to the toy store and bought back the boat which belonged to his son in the first place. He redeemed the boat and returned it to its rightful place. "That," says Barnhouse, "is redemption."

Redemption has several "dictionary" meanings coming from different Greek words that are all translated "grace." First, it can mean "to purchase from the marketplace." But it can also mean not only to purchase us from the market, but "to take us out of the market place." So, in relation to our salvation, it means that not only did Christ pay the price for our sin, but also removed us from the "marketplace" of sin.

A third thing it can mean is to pay a ransom, so that the held one can be freed.

And if you address as Father the One who impartially judges according to each man's work, conduct yourselves in fear during the time of your stay upon earth; knowing that you were not redeemed (*lutrao*) with perishable things like silver or gold from your futile way of life inherited from your forefathers, but with precious blood, as of a lamb unblemished and spotless, the blood of Christ (1 Peter 1:17–19 NASB).

So, when we take all three of these meanings together to form a composite picture of redemption, we see that by Christ's death on the cross, believers in Him have been, one, purchased; two, removed from the marketplace of sin; and three, set free to live a new life.

No human could pay the price for another person's sins, because the one who would volunteer to pay the price for another would himself deserve to die. A loving husband or father might want to die to save the life of a wife or child. But since the husband or father would himself deserve to die because of his own sin, his death could not be substituted for another. In Psalm 49:7 we read, "None of them can by any means redeem his brother, nor give to God a ransom for him. . . ."

The only one who could pay the price for another's death is someone who did not deserve to die. The only person who ever lived who fit that description is Jesus. Because He was a perfect man, He could die in the place of another. Because He was God, His death had infinite measure; it could count for countless others. As many as believe in Him and receive Him as their personal savior can have His death be a substitute for their own. Jesus can redeem all who will come to Him.

Jesus, then, provided for our forgiveness, our regeneration, and our justification, all working together to accomplish our redemption. And considering the alternative, what a fortunate thing that was for man. *Humanity outside of Christ is in a perilous situation.* Jesus did not die on the cross for nothing. The Son of God did not leave heaven, live a life of rejection and humiliation, die a physically excruciating death, and have all the sins of the world placed on His holy head for nothing, or for a lark, or to be one option among many. He did all this because it is the only way the redemption of humankind could be achieved. Man deserved to die because of his sin, and the only way that condition could be remedied was for someone who did not deserve to die to die in man's place.

In his book, *Who Is This Jesus?*, Michael Green writes:

> This is something we willfully ignore. It is too embarrassing. We love to play Jesus off against other faiths, or say, "Well, I can get to God my own way." The Cross puts a full stop to such folly. It tells us that we cannot get to God our own way. How can a bunch of rebels waltz back into the divine presence singing, "I did it my way"? The human race is in dire peril. Not only from international, social, economic, and ecological disasters. But from one more fundamental. We are out of touch with God, and most of us want to keep it that way (70).

It is not easy for people to admit that they are in eternal peril because their lives do not measure up to God's standards. Our "I'm OK, you're OK" mindset just doesn't make acknowledging our peril politically correct thinking. Like a drunk who doesn t have a job and has wracked up a $1,000,000 gambling bill which he will never be able to pay, so we have a debt of sin against God which we will never be able to pay. We have one hope. To have the debt forgiven. That is what Jesus does. He makes it possible for us to be forgiven.

The man who led me to me Lord died several years before the writing of this book. If you travel north about a mile out of the little farming community in Northern Indiana in which he lived his entire life, you come to a small, well-kept country cemetery. In that little cemetery, you will find a modest headstone which reads "Jake Berger—Forgiven." He could not have picked one word that said more. He understood the essence of salvation, the essence of reconciliation with God.

As the little chorus goes, "He paid a debt He did not owe, we owed a debt we could not pay." We have one hope: Forgiveness. And that hope lies in Jesus. No, His life was not meaningless. His was not the futile eruption of an overzealous optimist. He was God, who came to earth and became a man and died in our place. Because of that, we can know God and be with Him forever. How wonderful! What words can we use to say "Thank You" to God? What can we do to show our appreciation? Giving back to Him the life we owe is the only measure complete enough.

Speed Bump!

Slow down long enough to be sure you've gotten the main points of this chapter.

Question **Q1.** What did Jesus reveal to us about God's love for us?

Answer **A1.** Jesus revealed that God's love is so great that *nothing* can keep us from God if we will but come to Him.

Q2. What did Jesus reveal about how to live?

A2. Jesus revealed that life is to be lived in total *trust* in, and *obedience* to, our heavenly Father.

Q3. What did Jesus' life accomplish for our eternal destiny?

A3. Through Jesus we are *forgiven* of our sins, *reconciled* to God, and *made ready* for heaven.

Fill In the Blank

Question **Q1.** What did Jesus reveal to us about God's love for us?

Answer **A1.** Jesus revealed that God's love is so great that _____ can keep us from God if we will but come to Him.

Q2. What did Jesus reveal about how to live?

A2. Jesus revealed that life is to be lived in total _____ in, and _____ to, our heavenly Father.

Q3. What did Jesus' life accomplish for our eternal destiny?

A3. Through Jesus we are _____ of our sins, _____ to God, and _____ for heaven.

For Further Thought and Discussion

1. How would you evaluate this statement: How good you are has nothing whatsoever to do with whether or not you go to heaven.

2. How would you evaluate this statement: The opposite of obedience is unbelief. (If you don't obey, it is because you don't believe, or don't trust God)

3. How would you evaluate this statement: There is nothing we can do to make God love us less and there is nothing we can do to make God love us more.

What If I Don't Believe?

If I don't believe what Jesus accomplished, the consequences are much the same as the ones that were mentioned in previous chapters. We are at odds with the Bible, we deny either the need for salvation or the possibility of salvation, we lose all hope for guidance in this life and for life after death, and we have no encouraging words to share with others who are seeking the answers to life's most difficult questions.

For Further Study

1. Scriptures
Several passages in the Bible speak of what Jesus accomplished. They include:

- Ephesians 1:1–14

- 1 Peter 1:3–5

- John 3:16–18

- Ephesians 4:1

- 1 John 3:2–3

- Galatians 2:20

- Romans 5:1

2. Books
Several other books are very helpful in studying this subject. They are listed below in general order of difficulty. If I could only read one of these, I would read the first one.

Who Is This Jesus? Michael Green
More Than a Carpenter, Josh McDowell
The Words and Works of Jesus Christ, J. Dwight Pentecost

An agnostic found himself in trouble, and a friend suggested he pray. "How can I pray when I do not know whether or not there is a God?" he asked. "If you are lost in the forest," his friend replied, "you do not wait until you find someone before shouting for help."

6

Who Can Know Jesus?

It is extremely hard to get to know someone whom you cannot see, hear, smell, taste or touch. With those five senses we take in information from the world around us, and use them to get to know others. We rely primarily on seeing family and friends, hearing them and touching them. So how do we get to know someone who doesn't talk back? How do we get to know someone who has no body language which we can see to interpret? How do we get to know someone who does not give us a hug when we walk through the door, or pat us on the back when we have done something well? How do we get to know someone who lived two thousand years ago, and hasn't been seen since?

Well, one analogy might be getting to know someone through correspondence. My wife and I wrote letters back and forth for a number of months to each other my first year in theological seminary. In some ways, that helped us get to know each other better than if we were seeing each other face to face, because there is a level of communication that can come through in letters that often does not come through in face to face interaction. We often ask deeper, more personal questions than we would face to face. We might talk about longings, hopes, dreams or convictions in letters when we tend not to face to face. We often feel awkward discussing certain things, or talking about certain things, or saying certain things personally, which we feel quite comfortable doing in letters. For that reason, even in the age of ATT-MCI-Sprint competition and discounts, I am still a letter writer. I think it affords a deeper level of communication than can often be experienced personally.

But even then, I am not sure that writing letters is the best analogy for how to get to know Jesus, the One who does not write back to us.

Sometimes we feel we become acquainted with famous people from reading their books or listening to them speak. I feel I know several prominent Christian authors and radio speakers very well. I know about their families, I know what kinds of vacations they like, I know what kind of personalities they have, much of their value system, their commitment to Christ, and many other things.

I hesitate to mention names, but perhaps I am safe mentioning Billy Graham. I have read two of Billy Graham's biographies, I have heard him preach innumerable times, have read many articles about him, have seen him on television at affairs of national concern such as the swearing in of presidents, at marriages and deaths of prominent people, and so forth. I admire his integrity and leadership. He has had the same team around him for nearly fifty years! William McKay, a businessman and best-selling author in Minneapolis who does business with the Billy Graham organization, but who does not profess in his books to be a Christian, praises the integrity of Graham's organization and the excellence with which they conduct their business. I know about Graham's sense of humor, his penchant for dreading things that probably will not happen (every headache is a brain tumor, every bump of turbulence in an airplane a prelude to a crash). I know about his "aw-shucks" self-deprecation. I know about his children, which ones gave him particular problems growing up, and about his remarkable wife who has a mind of her own. I know much about him, and yet, that is not what it means to know Jesus, even though there are some parallels. Billy Graham doesn't know I am alive. I cannot talk to him, as I can to Jesus. Jesus knows me back. He always knows where I am because He never leaves me.

In this chapter we learn that:

1. We can meet Jesus by believing in Him, accepting Him as our Savior, repenting of our old life, and giving our lives over to Him.
2. We can grow in our knowledge of Christ by learning well the Scriptures, with a compliant heart.
3. We get to know Jesus better by imitating His example of living, emulating other good Christians, and observing our own spiritual experience.

Let me suggest another analogy, because there is no one analogy of what it means to know Jesus. Many thousands of men who became prisoners of war in Vietnam ended up in a prison camp in Hanoi called the "Hanoi Hilton." It was truly a hole of perdition, a death camp, a house of pain. And yet, many men lived through years of suffering there. How did they do it? Different people used different ways. Hope had to be kept alive. Many men coped by visualizing in exacting detail certain things they would do when they got out. Some people mentally played the piano. Others imagined themselves playing golf. Still others had assorted mental hobbies. All of them visualized being reunited with people they knew and loved. But one other thing was common to them all. A Morse-code communication system existed in the prison cells. When the guards would lock the prisoners up for the night and go to their quarters, the men would pass information back and forth by tapping on the walls. You did not know who was passing the information along, you could not see them, but you knew they were there and they knew you were there. They gave you life-giving and life-saving information. They gave you support when you were lonely or beaten and tortured. You knew they cared about you, even though they were not in a position to deliver you from your circumstances.

No, this is not what it means to get to know Jesus, because He taps out nothing to us on a daily basis that is personalized to us. But by combining these three examples, we can talk about who can know Jesus, and how to know Him.

How Can We Meet Jesus?

We meet Jesus by believing in Him, accepting Him as our Savior, repenting of our old life and giving our lives over to Him.

Back in the '50s a group of missionaries, including Nate Saint and Jim Elliot, decided to make contact with the Auca Indians in the remote wilderness of Ecuador, to bring the gospel to them. They located a village by air, and then dropped gifts to them from the airplane. Believing that these gifts had paved the way for a friendly contact with the Aucas, the missionaries returned to civilization, for there was no place to land an airplane in the wilderness, and canoed to the village. The Aucas, of course, were intrigued by the gifts, and seemed to be responding positively to the contacts. However, because of the twisted values of their own culture, they did not trust the missionaries, and one day killed the very ones who came with the desire and ability to do great good for them. In the providence of God, other missionaries made further contact, a friendly relationship was established, and the Aucas eventually converted to Christ in great numbers, including the specific individuals who killed the original missionaries.

This story remarkably parallels meeting Christ. Christ brought the gospel to humankind, but because of our twisted values, we did not understand or accept Him, and we killed Him, the very one who came with the desire and ability to do great good for us. But there is another parallel, which is the one I want to focus on. We are addressing the question, "How can we meet Jesus?" *We meet Jesus the same way the Auca Indians met their missionaries. Jesus initiates the meeting.*

Jesus initiates our meeting Him.   Jesus comes to us bearing gifts and evidence of His presence. We look at nature, and see the hand of God. We look within our own hearts, and something in there tells us that God exists. When we respond to the light He gives us in nature and conscience, He then gives us more light. If we respond again, He gives us more, and then more, until finally we meet Jesus.

Several key Scripture passages teach us this. First, is John 3:16–21:

> For God so loved the world that He gave His only begotten Son, that whoever believes in Him should not perish, but have everlasting life. For God did not send His Son into the world to condemn the world, but that the world through Him might be saved. He who believes in Him is not condemned; but he who does not believe is condemned already, because he has not believed in the name of the only begotten Son of God. And this is the condemnation, that the light has come into the world, and men loved darkness rather than light because their deeds were evil. For everyone practicing evil hates the light and does not come to the light, lest his deeds should be exposed. But he who does the truth comes to the light, that his deeds may be clearly seen, that they have been done in God.

In other words, those who want to find God follow the light He gives them until they find Him. This passage must be reinforced with John 6:44: "No one can come to Me unless the Father who sent Me draws him; and I will raise him up on the last day." Add to these 1 John 4:10: "In this is love, not that we loved God, but that He loved us and sent His Son {to be} the propitiation for our sins."

We see in these passages that we do not initiate the search for God. God initiates the search for us. When we "find" God, it is not really that we found Him. It is that we have simply responded to His overtures toward us, and He has drawn us to Himself.

Imagine two men trapped in a cave by an avalanche that covers the mouth of the cave. One man is an escaped convict, sentenced to death for murder. The other man is a hostage. They know they can never get out through the mouth of the cave where they entered, so they begin exploring the back of the cave in hope of finding a rear exit.

They search for hours, groping their way through the impenetrable blackness, stumbling over rubble, bumping into outcroppings in the walls. Finally, they come to a fork in the cave and must decide which fork to choose. Toward the left fork they see nothing but unending blackness. But when they look down the right fork, they can't believe their eyes! Far back they see a pinhead of light. Elated, they start scrambling for that dot of light. As they get closer to the light, they discover that the small pinhead is really a shaft of light shining into the cave. As they reach the shaft, they see it is streaming down from a hole large enough to

---

Why I need to know this

If I don't understand who can know Jesus, I am at risk of never knowing Him. If the Bible is true, unless I come to know Jesus, I will be separated from God forever when I die. Therefore, knowing Jesus is the single most important issue in life. Until I make the decision to receive Jesus and follow Him, all other decisions in life are secondary.

---

crawl out. But as they clamber toward the opening, they hear voices outside. It is the police. The hostage eagerly scrambles through the hole into broad daylight and is saved. The convict, not wanting to meet the police, retreats into the cave, hoping to find a way out that does not deliver him into the hands of the police. But there is no other exit. He dies in the cave.

The analogy? We are all lost in the cave of life, groping for a safe way out (hope for life after death.) In our groping, God shows each of us a pinhead of light. Those who want to find God can, by just following the light He gives them. First, the light of nature (Romans 1:18–20), then the light of conscience (Romans 2:12–16), next the light of Scripture, and finally the light of Jesus Himself (1 John 1:7). Those who do not want to meet Jesus turn their back on the light and walk further into the cave, hoping for another way out. There isn't one. They die in there.

Who can know Jesus? The one who, when he has walked toward the light, hears that Jesus is the Son of God, that he, himself is lost, destined for an eternity separated from God, and understands that only Jesus can save him from that destiny. He then believes in Jesus and commits his life to Him. Different factions of Christians use many words to describe this process. It is simple to say that he became a Christian. But that is so general that many people are unwilling to stop at that. Some say he is converted to Christ. Others say he is born again. Others say he becomes a believer. Still others say he receives Jesus as his personal savior. All of these are accurate if you understand what they mean. All of them can be misunderstood. The key, I think, is to try to use words that everyone can understand, and if there is chance of misunderstanding, to explain oneself.

Who can meet Jesus? The one who comes, by the grace and drawing of God, to understand and believe in who Jesus is, and gives himself over to Jesus.

How Can We Grow In Our Knowledge of Jesus Through the Scriptures?

We can grow in our knowledge of Christ by learning well the Scriptures, with a compliant heart.

The point at which someone becomes a follower of Christ is a beginning, not an end. At that point, you can say you know Christ in the same sense that you can say you know your new neighbor after having just met him. But there is a deeper, a wider, a more complete knowing of another person. If you spend any time with your neighbor as you live next door to him over the next twenty years, you will know your neighbor even better. The question we want to pursue, then, is how can we know Christ in this deeper, wider, more complete way?

There is a very strong link between the Bible and Jesus. The Bible is called the Word of God (Hebrews 4:12). In addition, Jesus is called the Word of God:

And I saw heaven opened; and behold, a white horse, and He who sat upon it is called Faithful and True; and in righteousness He judges and wages war. And His eyes are a flame of fire, and upon His head are many diadems; and He has a name written upon Him which no one knows except Himself. And He is clothed with a robe dipped in blood; and His name is called The Word of God (Revelation 19:11–13 NASB).

To know the Word is to know Jesus. To respect the Word is to respect Jesus. To study the Word is to study Jesus. To obey the Word is to obey Jesus. Who can get to know Jesus better? The one who gets to know the Word better. We are not talking about merely becoming familiar with facts in the Bible. Even the demons believe—and tremble (James 2:19). Many monsters of history such as Stalin and Hitler were said to have known large portions of the Bible. The one who knows Christ studies the Word with a view toward learning and understanding better who He is and what He desires of us. The one who studies with a compliant heart is the one who knows Christ richly.

Obedience is a concept much misunderstood and no longer popular today. Yet, obedience and knowing God walk hand in hand. You cannot know God, you cannot know Jesus well, unless you willingly obey the commands you read in Scripture and follow the example you see Him set in Scripture. In the fifteenth chapter of the Gospel of John, Jesus made clear the link between knowing Him and keeping His commandments:

The Scriptures teach us God's ways.

> If you abide in Me, and My words abide in you, ask whatever you wish, and it shall be done for you. By this is My Father glorified, that you bear much fruit, and so prove to be My disciples. Just as the Father has loved Me, I have also loved you; abide in My love. If you keep My commandments, you will abide in My love; just as I have kept My Father's commandments, and abide in His love. These things I have spoken to you, that My joy may be in you, and that your joy may be made full. This is My commandment, that you love one another, just as I have loved you. Greater love has no one than this, that one lay down his life for his friends. *You are My friends, if you do what I command you* (John 15:7–14, emphasis added NASB).

"You are my friends if you do what I command you." If you want friendship with Jesus, if you want to know Him intimately, you must obey. But be sure not to miss the blessing that follows obedience. If we keep His commandments, we abide in Him. When we abide in Him, He pours *His* joy into us and our own joy expands.

Jesus is not talking about fist-clenching, teeth-gritting obedience. He is talking about what Paul called in Romans 6:17 obedience from the heart. That brings us deeper knowledge of Jesus: A spirit of obedience from the heart as we learn His word.

How Can We Grow In Our Knowledge of Jesus Through Experience?

We get to know Jesus better by imitating His example of living, emulating other good Christians, and observing our own spiritual experience.

Jesus' Example

The Bible teaches us that Jesus' life is recorded in Scripture for our example, that we should follow Him (1 Peter 2:21), that we should imitate other more mature Christians (Hebrews 13:7), and that we should study our own lives to learn as much as we can about growing in Him (2 Timothy 2:15).

Let's examine each of these examples. First, we can study Jesus' behavior, and feel confident emulating it. For example, when Jesus was mistreated, He did not mistreat others in return. He returned goodness for evil. So when we are mistreated, we are to imitate Jesus, and not mistreat others in return.

The Example of Other Christians

I have been so impressed with the life of Chuck Colson, who is founder of Prison Fellowship, a ministry of evangelism and discipleship to prisoners and their families around the world. He has become an international spokesman for evangelical Christians in the last twenty years. Colson was special counsel for President Nixon during the Watergate Scandal which lead to the resignation of Nixon in 1974. Many people went to jail over the Watergate Scandal, which included the burglary of the Democratic National Committee Headquarters and a subsequent coverup which Nixon apparently participated in. Colson was not a Christian when the scandal hit, but became a Christian before the cases involving various Nixon adminstration officials came to trial. He was examined to determine any guilt in the scandal. He was exonerated of any guilt in the Watergate scandal, but felt that he needed to "come clean" before God for other things he had done. Under oath, Colson volunteered information on other illegal things he had been involved in. Had he simply kept quiet and answered only the questions which were asked of him, he would have gotten away with everything. But because he became a Christian between the time he committed the crimes and the trials, he felt he was under obligation to God to voluntarily admit to his wrongdoings. As a result, he went to prison of his own free will, because of a spirit of obedience to Christ. I see such commitment and dedication in another Christian, and it inspires me to be more committed and dedicated to Christ.

Personal Reflections

Finally, we are to monitor our own spiritual development. Jesus promises that He will keep us fed, clothed and sheltered. It may not be in the manner to which we have been accustomed, but He didn't guarantee that. But as we pray, asking Him to show Himself strong on our behalf by making His promises come true for us, and then watch Him keep those promises, our confidence in Him grows, and we get to know Him. We learn that we can rely on Him. As we obey His commands, often with fear and trembling at first, we discover that He meets our needs and His grace is sufficient for us. That convinces us to trust Him in the future.

This principle is seen in the Old Testament. God does stupendous miracles for Israel. One very clear example is when the Israelites where camped on the east side of the Jordan River near the city of Jericho. The river was at flood stage, and there was no way for the Israelites to cross over. God miraculously caused the waters to part, and allowed them to cross over on the dry river bed. When they got on the other side, Joshua commanded that twelve large stones be taken from the river bed and put in a pile on the west side to form a memorial to that event. Then, when future generations ask what the stones mean, the older generation can say, those stones are a memorial to God's faithfulness in bringing us into the promised land.

We need to do the same thing in our personal life. We can record the things God does for us, review them occasionally, and remind ourselves of them. It makes it easier to trust God in the future. We get to know Jesus more fully by observing how He worked in our lives in the past so that we can trust Him more readily in the future.

This can be done several ways. I keep a special card file of my urgent prayer requests. When a truly mountainous issue looms

before me, I note the prayer request on a card. Since I reserve
these for the truly (to me) critical things, I don t have more than

**Spiritual growth
results from
following scriptural
examples.**

seven or eight cards in the file. When the request is answered, I write the answer on the
other side of the card. It is truly encouraging to
see how God responds when life pinches hard.
He usually answers differently from the way I
expected, but always His grace is sufficient.

Of course, the same kind of thing can be done on a lesser scale
by keeping a prayer log. In a general prayer log, you jot down all
your requests, and write down all the answers. This also gives
you a feel for how God works in your life.

A further idea is simply to keep a journal or diary. As you
thumb through it, you will see the work of God in your life even
though you didn't keep a specific log of prayers and answers.

As you look back, you realize that some things you thought
were critical really weren't. You see that God is not a genie, to answer our every wish whenever we rub the prayer bottle. Rather,
He is our sovereign Lord. He doesn't serve us; we serve Him.
And while God will never be reduced to an equation, these kinds
of observations of how God works in our life help us to understand Him and know Him better.

Who Can Know Jesus?

We started out asking the question, Who can know Jesus? The
answer is, from the human perspective, "Anyone." Whoever calls
upon the name of the Lord will be saved. Whoever comes to Him,
He certainly will not cast out. He invites you to come to Him to
have your sins forgiven, to have your spirit reborn, to give you a
new purpose and power in life, and to make you ready for
heaven.

It seems only reasonable at this point to ask if you, the reader,
have converted to Christ. Do you believe He is the Son of God?
Do you agree that you are a sinner, incapable of saving yourself?
Do you want to live with God forever in heaven? Do you want
Him to guide your life, give you meaning in life, and the confi-
dence of being loved? Are you willing to give your life over to
Him, to be obedient to Him to the best of your ability?

If you believe and want these things, then tell God in your
own words. Simply acknowledge your sinfulness and repent of it.
Tell Him that you believe in Him and want Him to come into

your life and make you into the kind of person He wants you to be (and the kind of person you want to be). Tell Him that you want to give your life to Him, and that you want to go to heaven when you die. If you tell God that sincerely, then the Bible assures you that, having come to Christ, He did not cast you out. Having called upon the name of the Lord, you were saved. Having believed in Him and received Him, you are now a child of God.

Many people have done something like this earlier in their lives, but strayed away from the Lord, and now are not sure if they are still Christians. If you have any doubt, the only sensible thing to do is go through the process again and remove all doubt. Tell the Lord these things again, and be sure that you belong to Him. Then give your life to Him in obedience from the heart, to learn as much as you can of Jesus from the Scripture and from observing how He works in your life and the lives of others. You can know Christ. It is not easy. The Bible says it is a glory for God to conceal a matter, and a glory for kings to search the matter out. God does not make the Christian life a breeze but He is the shelter in the storm. As we pursue our God, we learn to recognize His footprints, and get to know Him better as we walk in the light with Him.

Speed Bump!

Slow down long enough to be sure you've gotten the main points of this chapter.

---

*Q*uestion
*A*nswer

Q1. How can we meet Jesus?

A1. By *believing* in Him, accepting Him as our Savior, repenting of our old life and giving our lives over to Him.

Q2. How can we grow in our knowledge of Jesus through the Scriptures?

A2. We can grow in our knowledge of Christ by *learning* well the Scriptures, with a compliant heart.

Q3. How can we grow in our knowledge of Jesus through experience?

A3 We get to know Jesus better by *imitating* His example of living, emulating other good Christians, and observing our own spiritual experience.

Fill In the Blank

*Q*uestion
*A*nswer

Q1. How can we meet Jesus?

A1. By _____ in Him, accepting Him as our Savior, repenting of our old life and giving our lives over to Him.

Q2. How can we grow in our knowledge of Jesus through the Scriptures?

A2. We can grow in our knowledge of Christ by _____ well the Scriptures, with a compliant heart.

Q3. How can we grow in our knowledge of Jesus through experience?

A3. We get to know Jesus better by _____ His example of living, emulating other good Christians, and observing our own spiritual experience.

For Further Thought and Discussion

1. Before reading this chapter, what would you have said if someone had asked you what a Christian was? Now that you have read this chapter, how would you answer?

2. So many people think you get to heaven by being a good person, but how good would you have to be? We have seen in other chapters that being good is not enough; we must be perfect, and we can only become perfect through Christ. But once we have become a Christian, why does it matter whether or not we try to live a good life?

3. If you look up to another Christian as a model, and he does something terrible like commit adultery, what would you tell yourself to keep it from destroying your faith?

4. How can it be fair of God to expect us to use Christ as an example for our lives since He is perfect and we are not?

What If I Don't Believe?

This chapter talks the most clearly about what it means to be a Christian and how to become one. If I don t believe it, it means that until I change my mind, I am not a Christian.

If I don't believe that I can learn more of Christ by studying His Word with a compliant heart, then I am locked into trying to live without the help of Scriptures, which is like trying to sail the seas without a compass. It also means that, if I do not have a compliant heart toward the truth, I am liable to have a very difficult time getting along in life, because life demands a compliant heart if we are to have good relationships with others.

If I don't believe that I can learn more about Christ by imitating His example as well as the example of others, I will not have the benefit of the best way to learn how to live successfully, and that is by imitation. I may end up having little respect for others, and fail to benefit from the influence of good people in my life.

For Further Study

1. Scripture
Several passages speak of how we can know Jesus. They include:

- John 1:12
- John 3:16–18
- Ephesians 2:1–10
- 2 Timothy 3:16–17
- Hebrews 4:12
- Hebrews 13:7

If you wish further study, read these passages and consider how they contribute to your understanding of the subject of this chapter.

2. Books
Several other books are very helpful in studying further this subject. They are listed below in general order of difficulty. If I could only read one of these, I would read the first one:

How To Be Born Again, Billy Graham
30 Days to Understanding How To Live as a Christian, Max Anders
Loving God, Charles Colson

I believe in Christianity as I believe in the sun—
not only because I see it, but because by it I see
everything else.
■ **C.S. Lewis**

7

Why Believe Jesus Ever Lived?

If you were born after 1950, you might not know the story of *Ben Hur*. This classic book written by a Civil War general, Lew Wallace, in 1899, was turned into a movie starring Charleton Heston, which won the Academy Award for best movie in 1959. It is a towering story of love, of suffering, of the struggle of good against evil, and finally of triumph. Judah Ben Hur, the story's hero, grows up with his boyhood friend, Marsalla. They are ancient, Mideastern Tom Sawyer and Huck Finn. Judah is, of course, a Jew, and Marsalla, a Gentile. Judah is the heir of a very great and wealthy house in Jerusalem. Marsalla is a promising military man who trained in Rome as a soldier, then returned to Jerusalem as the leader of the Roman occupation forces.

During a parade, a tile falls from the roof of Judah Ben Hur's house and strikes the new Roman ruler of the area. Judah is falsely arrested and sent to row as a slave in a Roman military ship. Marsalla knew it was an accident and could have prevented Judah's arrest, but because of his lust for power, didn't. In addition, Judah's mother and sister are imprisoned in Jerusalem.

Judah hates Marsalla, and while in the belly of the military ship, providing the power for naval warfare, he vows that he will live, return to Jerusalem and free his mother and sister. Slaves in such ships rarely lived for more than a year. Judah had been rowing for three years when, in the heat of a naval battle, his ship was sunk. He saved the commander of the ship, and as a reward, was given his freedom and adopted by the commander, who was the top naval officer in the Roman navy, a very powerful and wealthy man.

He returns to Jerusalem with all the wealth and power of his new identity, and confronts the astonished Marsalla, who assumed he had been dead for years. Ben Hur demanded that Marsalla find and release from prison his mother and sister. Marsalla finds them in prison, but they have leprosy, so he whisks them away to the leper colony outside Jerusalem to live out a pitiful existence. Ben Hur is told that they are dead. His hate for Marsalla grows, and in a chariot race in which Marsalla and Judah Ben Hur are the primary figures, Marsalla is killed. With his dying breath, Marsalla, out of spite, tells Judah the truth about his mother and sister.

Judah's hate now no longer has an object to focus on. He generalizes his hatred and becomes a bitter shell of his former self. Finally, in desperation he goes to the leper colony to get his mother and sister to take them to Jesus, this great preacher who has been performing miracles. When they get to Jerusalem where they think they will find Him, they discover that He has just been crucified. Now, all hope is gone, and despair settles over them. However, in the hours after Jesus' crucifixion, when the day turned to night, and storms and earthquakes rocked the city, Judah's mother and sister are healed of the leprosy, and Judah's heart, along with his mother's and sister's, is turned to Jesus. Their faith, their health and their lives are restored.

In this chapter we examine one decision and three kinds of evidence critical to our view about whether or not Jesus ever lived:

1. We make our decision about who Jesus is by letting the evidence speak for itself to our open mind, or by deciding ahead of time that the evidence cannot be believed.
2. More evidence supports the historical existence of Jesus than any other figure of antiquity.
3. Evidence from secular writers contemporary with Jesus is scant, but several key and convincing sources exist.
4. Very early archaeological evidence, like early historical references, is not overabundant, but is highly credible.

It is a towering story, deeply moving, and an exquisite portrayal of the power, grace and love of Jesus. Why did I tell you about Ben Hur? Because of this interesting twist. As Paul Harvey would say, this is "the rest of the story." When Lew Wallace set out to study the life of Christ, he was not a Christian. In fact, writing a story such as Ben Hur was the farthest thing from his mind. Wallace was antagonistic toward Christianity, and determined he would study the life of Christ so thoroughly, and then write so convincingly, that he would be able to kill the story of Christ. He wanted to prove that Jesus, if He had lived, was not God, but merely a man, that He never rose from the dead, and that Christianity was a hoax.

So he studied. This great and enormous subject drew him further and further into his research until the evidence overwhelmed him. He dropped to his knees and cried out to Jesus to be his Savior and Lord. Then, instead of writing a book to prove to the world that Jesus was not God, he wrote *Ben Hur*, to try to prove to the world that Jesus was God.

Other Skeptics Who Believed

Lew Wallace is not the only one who has tried to disprove the deity and claims of Christ through scholarly research and ended up convinced by the evidence that Jesus was God. Frank Morison wrote an extremely important book entitled, *Who Moved the Stone*. He had intended to strip Christianity of its "overgrowth of primitive beliefs" and present the "real" Jesus. Once he confronted the evidence, however it overwhelmed him, and he wrote a book demonstrating reasons why the resurrection was true. In a masterful approach, he takes all the possible explanations for the resurrection and demonstrates how each of them could not be true, and that the only historically viable explanation is that Jesus of Nazareth rose from the dead.

The halls of history are lined with people who decided they would get rid of Jesus, and ended up crying out to Him for salvation. Truth, you see, need fear no examination. The brighter the light shined on it, the more it is revealed to be truth.

C.S. Lewis, a British scholar who taught at Oxford and Cambridge, in his autobiographical book *Surprised by Joy* tells his own account of coming to faith in Christ. He says that he did not want to come to Christ. Emotionally, he was dead set against it. But the evidence kept compelling him to drop his prejudices and draw nearer and nearer. Then, one night, something catastrophic happened:

> While I was teaching at Magdalene College at Oxford University, early in 1926, the hardest boiled of all the atheists I ever knew sat in my room on the other side of the fire and remarked that the evidence for the historical accuracy of the Gospels was really surprisingly good. "Rum thing. Rum thing. It almost looks as if it had really happened once." To understand the shattering impact of it, you would need to know the man (who has certainly never since shown any interest in Christianity). If he, the cynic of cynics, the toughest of the tough were not—as I would still have put it—"safe," where could I turn? Was there no escape?

Later, you must picture me alone in that room at Magdalene, night after night, feeling, whenever my mind lifted even for a second from my work, the steady, unrelenting hand of Him whom I so earnestly desired not to meet. That which I greatly feared had at last come upon me. In the Trinity Term of 1929, I gave in, and admitted that God was God, and knelt and prayed: perhaps, that night, the most dejected and reluctant convert in all England (223–224, 228–229).

Why I need to know this

If I don't know the evidence for believing that Jesus was a real, historical figure, I may be intimidated by those who claim that He wasn't. We are often unnecessarily crippled by ignorance in our defense of the faith. We can confidently demonstrate that the evidence for the historical existence of Jesus is as good or better than that for any other ancient figure.

Most of us, however, have never heard or read the evidence for believing that Jesus actually lived. One day, when I was a young teenager, my cousin asked me, "How do we know that the Bible is really true? How do we know that the disciples didn't make it all up?" That question intimidated me because I had never thought about it. I had grown up in church believing everything I was taught, and it had never occurred to me to question that Jesus actually lived. I trusted my teachers, and assumed that the whole thing couldn't have gotten this far without someone uncovering it if it were a scam. In the end, my assumption proved correct. If it had been a scam, someone would have uncovered it long ago. Plenty of people, Wallace and Lewis included, would have uncovered it if it had not been true.

But, what is the evidence? What do we know? What information did Lew Wallace and C.S. Lewis come across that was so compelling to them, that convinced them of so many things, beginning with the fact that Jesus of Nazareth was an historical figure? He really lived.

How Do We Make Our Decision About Who We Believe Jesus Is?

We make our decision about who Jesus is by letting the evidence speak for itself to our open mind, or by deciding ahead of time that the evidence cannot be believed.

We have two choices in deciding what we believe about Jesus. We decide that it is possible that He existed, and we let the evidence suggest to us the probability of whether or not He did. Or we decide ahead of time that He did not exist, and we pick and choose what we want to believe, depending on whether or not it supports the decision we have already made before looking at any evidence. To a sympathetic reader this seems absurd, yet some people chose not to believe that Jesus lived simply because they don't want to believe that He lived. Belief that He lived would interfere with their lifestyles. His very presence demands a response.

This is a very foolish position. Truth is truth, regardless of what you think of it or how you treat it. Truth remains untouched and unchanged, regardless of whether or not it is believed. So the wisest policy is to go into any study with an open mind and let the evidence determine what is true and what is not true.

What Does the Evidence Suggest About the Life of Jesus?

More evidence supports the historical existence of Jesus than any other figure of antiquity.

If we accept the tests to determine the existence of Julius Caesar, Constantine, or Alexander the Great, and apply those tests in an unbiased manner to Jesus, we conclude that Jesus lived. If we deny the existence of Jesus, then to be consistent we must also deny the existence of Julius Caesar, Constantine, and Alexander the Great.

The evidence we have concerning the beginning of Christianity, its early beliefs, and its spread is best explained by agreeing that Jesus was a real historical figure. And virtually no historians suggest that Jesus did not exist. Denying the existence of Jesus requires wrenching the evidence out of its socket and manipulating it to point to any other conclusion. There have been, and probably always will be, those who say that Jesus never lived, and they will continue to provide straws for people to grasp at who don't want to believe in Him. As Alister McGrath points out, "The fact remains that those people are not taken seriously by impartial historical scholarship" (*Understanding Jesus*, 18).

What Secular Evidence Do We Have of Jesus' Existence?

Evidence from secular writers contemporary with Jesus is scant, but several key and convincing sources exist.

Jesus was not a prominent figure except to the Jews around Jerusalem and the sea of Galilee, and the immediate Roman rulers of that area who were interested in keeping a guerrilla uprising from occurring among the radical Jews. The average person outside Judea and Galilee, the Roman provinces roughly corresponding to modern Israel, would not know of Jesus. His crucifixion was a disagreeable form of capital punishment that a cultured non-Jewish society would have recoiled from. It would be much like a hanging today. Few of us would have the stomach to give much attention to a hanging, and would assume that anyone hanged was an unimportant person. There was simply no reason to write about Him until the number of people who began following Him after His crucifixion and "alleged" resurrection became great enough to warrant public attention. The average person who knew about His crucifixion assumed that that was the end of it. Even His disciples believed that; they went back to their fishing! Only when He "didn't go away," when the number of people who claimed He was still alive and followed Him grew from hundreds to thousands to tens of thousands, that history began to pay any attention to this carpenter-turned-teacher from Galilee.

Nevertheless, some very early non-Christian writers do mention Him. We will focus on three primary historians who are best known. The first two are Roman senators and historians whose lives overlapped the apostle John's: Cornelius Tacitus and Gaius Plinius Caecilius Secundus (not one of your more popular names today). Essentially, he was *Pliny, Jr.* Tacitus was born somewhere around A.D. 55, distinguished himself as a great orator, and died sometime after A.D. 116. Pliny the Younger was born around A.D. 61 and died around A.D. 110. He was a successful lawyer, diplomat, and a polished gentleman. He wrote in lofty Latin of events of social and historical significance.

Tacitus

First we look at the writings of Tacitus, an early Roman historian, writing around A.D. 115. He writes of the key events of the reigns of the Roman emperors up to his time. In A.D. 64, a vast section of Rome burned to the ground. The prevailing view is that Nero, a neurotic egomaniac, wanted to create an architectural renaissance in Rome, and burned down a large area in the center of the city for his palace and other grand buildings. Whether that was true or not, we do not know for sure, but the rumor prevailed. Tacitus writes in his Annals:

> To dispel the rumor, Nero substituted as culprits and treated with the most extreme punishments, some people popularly known as Christians, whose disgraceful activities were notorious. The originator of the name, Christ, had been executed when Tiberius was emperor by order of the procurator Pontius Pilate. But the deadly cult, though checked for a time, was now breaking out again not only in Judea, the birthplace of this evil, but even throughout Rome where all nasty and disgusting ideas from all over the world pour in and find a ready following (15.44).

Tacitus obviously had no love in his heart for Christianity, but this account does verify a number of historical events. Namely, that Jesus lived, that He was from Judea, lived during the reign of Tiberius (A.D. 14–37), and was executed by Pontius Pilate, who governed the province of Judea from A.D. 26–36. These dates all match the biblical record, yet, Tacitus would not likely be using biblical records for his information, considering the disdain with which he mentioned Christianity and Christ. He would be using Roman records. Further, he establishes that Jesus had a large following that was well-established in Rome by the time of Nero's reign in the sixties.

Tacitus referred to Christians again in his book *Histories*. This book does not exist any more, but an excerpt of it is found in another book in which the writer quotes Tacitus's *Histories*. In this book, Tacitus is quoted as saying that Christianity began as a sect within Judaism, though by this time it had become a separate and distinct movement, even frowned upon now by Judaism. He mentions the destruction of Jerusalem by the Emperor Tiberius in A.D. 70, and speculates that Titus destroyed the Jewish temple in Jerusalem, and hoped to wipe out both Christianity and Judaism by such total destruction. While we might wish that Tacitus had written more about Christianity and Christ, we must keep in mind that he very well may have, but that the writings were not preserved. He obviously wrote things of which we no longer have any record. He does give us what was, for a long time, the only secular mention of the existence of Pontius Pilate, and in doing so, lends great non-biblical credibility to the biblical story. More recently, two thirds of Pontius Pilate's name has been found in an inscription at Caesarea, a town on the Mediterranean coast in modern Israel.

Pliny

Pliny the Younger, another historian, governed Bithynia in Northern Turkey in A.D. 112. This area would have been first touched by Christianity through the travels of the apostle Paul. While under the authority of Emperor Trajan, Pliny wrote a rather lengthy letter about Christians and the trouble he was having governing Bithynia because of them. The sect was spreading rapidly throughout the entire region of what is today modern Turkey, and was becoming an economic problem, and therefore causing civil unrest. The pagan temples were closing down for want of customers, the pagan festivals were no longer being attended sufficiently for them to be continued with credibility, and the demand for sacrificial animals had virtually ceased, causing great economic hardship to those involved in providing goods and services to these pagan activities and institutions.

In a grisly act of desperation, Pliny executed those who openly admitted their Christianity, but he had an uneasy conscience. That is why he wrote to Trajan about them. He wanted guidance as to what to do. The Christians were doing nothing harmful. They had simply quit supporting the existing religion. He wrote that their lives were exemplary, that you would not find fraud, adultery, theft, or dishonesty among them.

The rumor had circulated that they practiced cannibalism during their own religious rituals, a distortion of the practice of communion in which Christians take bread and wine in ceremony as symbolic of the blood and body of Christ. Upon investigation, Pliny reported that at their "common meal" they ate food of an "ordinary and innocent kind." Through savage and needless persecution, Pliny was able to shore up the economy surrounding the pagan practices, and in doing so, ease the financial burden of Christianity on the area.

While Pliny gives us no information about Jesus Himself, it is clear that Christianity was a major movement in his part of the country, and no one doubts that the movement goes back to its founder, Jesus, who lived under Pontius Pilate during the reigns of Augustus Caesar and Tiberius.

Josephus

The third historian, Josephus, wrote somewhere around A.D. 70. He gives us the most powerful secular, contemporary reference to Jesus. Josephus was a Jew who fought to oppose the Roman presence in Jerusalem and Judea between A.D. 66 and 70. He was captured and brought before the Roman commander, Vespasian. Josephus, or Joseph, as was his Jewish name, was a shrewd man, clever at surviving. He boldly prophesied that Vespasian and his son Titus were to be emperors of Rome. Vespasian was so deeply impressed with this prophecy (probably because of his own superstition), that he kept Joseph alive until he could see whether or not the prophecy would come true.

It did. At the end of a civil disturbance involving factional fighting, Vespasian emerged as emperor of Rome. Joseph looked pretty good. So, Vespasian "latinized" Joseph, changing his name to Flavius Josephus. Flavius was Vespasian's household name, and Josephus, of course, is the Roman version of Joseph. From that time on, Josephus' destiny was secured. He set out to write a Jewish history, and from his biased reporting, evidently tried to restore the reputation of his countrymen for posterity. He mentions names which were common in the Bible: Herod the Great and Herod Antipas, Caiaphas, the high priest during Jesus' life. John the Baptist, and James "the brother of Jesus, the so-called Christ." Further, Josephus records the most extensive statement about Jesus found outside the Bible in his *Antiquities of the Jews*:

And about this time [meaning the governorship of Pontius Pilate], there appeared Jesus, a wiseman, if indeed he should be called a man, for he was the performer of amazing works, and a teacher of those who receive the truth with pleasure. He won over many Jews and many Greeks. He was the Messiah. Pilate, on the accusation of our leading men, condemned him to be crucified, but those who had first loved him did not give up. On the third day he appeared to them, alive again, for God's prophets had foretold this, and countless other astonishing things about him. And still to this day the race of Christians, named after him, has not died out (18.3.3).

Versions of this statement vary slightly, and certain words here and there have exception taken to them as to whether or not they were actually written by Josephus, and not by a Christian editor. But the statement as a whole stands up before secular classical scholars. For example, when Josephus calls Jesus the Messiah, it must be explained. Either Josephus meant it, in which case he would be declaring himself to be a Christian, which is unlikely. Or he was alluding to what other people said about Jesus, without making it clear that such was not his opinion. Or a Christian editor added the statement or amended an original one. But when all the secular scholarship is complete, even the secular scholars (not biblical scholars who might have a vested interest in the outcome of the study) say that the heart of the statement stands up. "As the lawyers say, 'The case rests' " (*Jesus Christ, Man or Myth*, E.M. Blaiklock, 31).

So powerful a testimony from a Jewish historian who would probably be antagonistic to Jesus and His followers is utterly reliable confirmation of the fundamental truths about Jesus and Christianity from a secular source which agrees with the biblical record. As Michael Green has noted,

It remains a solid, reliable statement by Josephus (whose life overlapped with Jesus) to the founder of Christianity, to His acceptance as the messiah, His wisdom, His teaching, His miracles, His many converts, His death, and His resurrection—not to mention the continued existence of His movement (*Who Is This Jesus?* 117–118).

Others

So far, we have looked at the three primary secular sources for information about the historically verifiable existence of Jesus. A number of other, less significant sources which are interesting to know about, bolster the secular evidence. One very early source even earlier than Pliny and Tacitus is a man named Thallus, a Samaritan, who wrote in Rome around A.D. 52. As a historian, he wrote that the darkness that came upon the earth when Jesus died on the cross was an eclipse of the sun. This is a brief but dramatic reference regarding an event (the darkness) which was well enough known that it could not be ignored.

Another brief but significant reference to Jesus came from Serapion, a Syrian, who was imprisoned (he felt unjustly), in the

A.D. 70's. This letter preserved in the British Museum, contains his reflections on what may happen to those who have imprisoned a just man without cause. He observes that in payment for killing Socrates, the Greeks received plague and famine, and that the Jews received the sacking of their city and the dispersion of their nation for the execution of their "wise King." His implication is that those who imprisoned him will receive their dreadful "just reward." For our intent, however, we notice that this is a reference to Jesus and His crucifixion, and to His claim to be the King of the Jews. Serapion, of course, was not a Chris-tian and would have no reason to advance the cause of Christianity. He was merely re-marking on something which was a generally known historical fact.

In addition, the rabbis of Jesus' time and shortly thereafter wrote about Him, which is not surprising. For the most part, they resented Him and tried to discredit Him during His earthly life and after.

These writings allude to his birth, which they acknowledge to be different. They allude, also, to His miracles: "he practiced magic and led Israel astray." They allude to His disciples, a close circle, one of whom was called Matthew. They allude to His death by crucifixion during the Jewish feast of the Passover. They even al-lude to His claim to share the nature of God and to be returning in judgment at the end of history (Green, 118).

What Archaeological Evidence Do We Have of Jesus' Life?

Very early archaeological evidence, like early historical references, is not overabundant, but is highly credible.

In this chapter, we are looking at historical evidence for the existence of Jesus of Nazareth, and we are including only the earliest evidence. Obviously, it would do no good to walk down to the corner of Main Street and Elm in your home town and point to the First Episcobapterian Church as archaeological evidence for the historical existence of Christ. If we are going do demon-strate that He really lived, we must get as close to His life as pos-sible. Therefore, while a massive amount of evidence going back only to A.D. 500, suggests the existence of Christ, we must dig fur-ther to see if, at the very root, the material we see in A.D. 500 is built on reality. As when all seeds germinate, the roots are very small, and grow only as the plant matures, so it is with Christianity. Massive archaeological evidence for the life of Christ in the first century after His death does not exist. Nevertheless, there is some. And, as the mighty oak comes from the lowly acorn, so the mighty presence of Christianity in the history of the world comes from lowly beginnings—but beginnings nevertheless.

1. Luke's Census. In Luke 2:1–5, we read that Caesar Augustus decreed that all the inhabited earth (Roman Empire) should be taxed, and that everyone had to return to his own city to pay the taxes. As a result, Mary and Joseph traveled to Bethlehem, Joseph's home town. The timing was such that Mary gave birth to Jesus in Bethlehem instead of in Nazareth, and thus was fulfilled the Old Testament prophecy. Archaeological evidence cited by Gary Habermas in *Ancient Evidence for the Life of Jesus* supports this census and the tax, during the time Jesus was born (152–153).

2. Yohanan, crucifixion victim. In June of 1968 while excavation was being done in Jerusalem to build a large apartment building, a burial site was unearthed. One of the people buried at the site had undergone crucifixion. A careful analysis of the skeleton revealed that his crucifixion was exactly the same kind that Jesus experienced, verifying the New Testament record of the way Jesus was crucified.

3. The Nazareth Decree. In 1878, a marble slab measuring approximately fifteen feet by twenty-four feet was discovered at Nazareth, describing itself as an "ordinance of Caesar." This Imperial edict calls for the death penalty on anyone who steals from tombs. The inscription belongs to the time of Tiberius (A.D. 14–37), or Claudius (A.D. 41–54). This decree was quite out of the ordinary, since grave robbing was very common, and not usually punishable by death. As scholars have tried to speculate what would account for such an extreme penalty for such a comparatively minor crime, it is difficult to escape several "coincidences."

First, it is dated during the general time Jesus was crucified. Second, it was found in Jesus' home town. Third, the sentence was unusually harsh. From these coincidences, it seems highly possible that this decree was a government reaction to the resurrection of Jesus, an event that profoundly embarrassed everyone responsible. This decree may have been a reaction to try to stop rumors of resurrections, since the Roman government would not likely have actually believed in the resurrection, but, knowing that others did, wanted to discourage the belief however possible.

4. Ancient Christian symbols. A small house church in Pompeii was destroyed in the eruption of Mt. Vesuvius. Marks on a wall clearly indicate where a cross had been hastily removed, probably a possession valued for either spiritual or monetary reasons, which the owner wanted to take with him as he ran for his life. Other Christian symbols have been found in the ruins of Pompeii, including a curious acrostic called the Rotas-Sator square. The complicated figure is difficult to decipher, but it is unarguably a Chris-tian symbol. These date back to A.D. 79, very close to the time of Christ, and during the life of the apostle John.

Well known among archaeological discoveries is the common use of the "fish" symbol, a simple outline used because the Greek word for fish was *Ichthus*. The Christians symbolically attributed a Greek word to each of its letters: *"Iesous Christos Theou Huios Soter,"* meaning, "Jesus Christ, Son of God, Savior." Until it became commonly known, it was a secret sign with which Christians could identify each other without non-Christians knowing it. When Christianity became lawful, it was used widely as a Christian symbol.

Finally, in 1945, Professor Sukenik, an Israeli archaeologist, found a sealed tomb just outside Jerusalem which had miraculously escaped having been robbed. The grave yielded coins dating to approximately A.D. 50, and five caskets with the name of Jesus written clearly on them. One reads "Jesus' help." Another reads "Jesus, let him arise." Charcoal crosses also clearly mark them. As with most archaeological finds, they are subject to different interpretations, but the Jewish professor's explanation is the most straightforward and probable; namely, that they are the earliest known allusions to Jesus by Christian believers. They date to within *twenty years* of the crucifixion itself.

Summary. As we said, very early archaeological evidence for the historical existence of Christ is not an overflowing archaeological flood. Christianity was an infant movement in the early days. Very little has survived from that era, let alone evidence for the existence of a rabbi who taught only for three years and was rejected by those to whom He preached. But though meager, this evidence is very important. When you combine the archaeological evidence with the written references from historians whose lives overlapped the life of Jesus, there is little room to interpret it any other way than that Jesus of Nazareth was a historical figure.

Speed Bump!

Slow down long enough to be sure you've gotten the main points of this chapter.

Question
Answer

Q1. How do we make our decision about who Jesus is?

A1. We make our decision about who Jesus is either by letting the *evidence* speak for itself to our open mind, or by deciding ahead of time that the evidence cannot be believed.

Q2. What does the evidence suggest about the life of Jesus?

A2. More evidence supports the historical *existence* of Jesus than any other figure of antiquity.

Q3. What secular evidence do we have of Jesus' existence?

A3. Evidence from secular writers contemporary with Jesus is scant, but several key and *convincing* sources exist.

Q4. What archaeological evidence do we have of Jesus' life?

A4. Very early archaeological evidence, like early historical references, is not overabundant, but is highly *credible*.

Fill In the Blank

Question
Answer

Q1. How do we make our decision about who Jesus is?

A1. We make our decision about who Jesus is either by letting the _____ speak for itself to our open mind, or by deciding ahead of time that the evidence cannot be believed.

Q2. What does the evidence suggest about the life of Jesus?

A2. More evidence supports the historical _____ of Jesus than any other figure of antiquity.

Q3. What secular evidence do we have of Jesus' existence?

A3. Evidence from secular writers contemporary with Jesus is scant, but several key and _____ sources exist.

Q4. What archaeological evidence do we have of Jesus' life?

A4. Very early archaeological evidence, like early historical references, is
not overabundant, but is highly _____.

For Further Thought and Discussion

1. How much do you think the typical person really knows before he
makes a decision to believe in or not believe in Jesus? What do you
think is the primary factor in most people's decision?

2. What do you think is the importance of knowing about secular
historical and archaeological evidence for the life of Christ?

3. Why do you think atheists and agnostics do not find historical evidence
for the life of Christ convincing, while other people do? If it is not a
matter of intellect or education, what accounts for it?

What If I Don't Believe?

1. If I don't believe Jesus ever lived, I run counter to the consensus of
history. Virtually no major historians doubt that someone named Jesus
of Nazareth lived.

2. I regard the disciplines of history and archaeology as either ignorant or
incompetent, since those disciplines as a whole support Jesus' existence.

3. I call into question the historical accuracy of most ancient figures, since
the existence of all ancient figures is determined by the same criteria as
Jesus'.

For Further Study

1. Scriptures
Several other Scripture passages speak of reasons to believe that Jesus
lived.

- Acts 5:30–39 (If there were nothing to it, it would have died out by now.)

- Romans 1:18–21 (God placed a knowledge of Him in our hearts, and
reinforced it through nature).

- Luke 2:1–5 (Such an obvious and easily verified historical incident which is central to prophecy and the life of Christ.)

2. Books

Several other books are very helpful in studying further this subject. They are listed below in general order of difficulty. If I could only read one of these, I would read the first one:

Who Is This Jesus? Michael Green
Ancient Evidence for the Life of Jesus, Gary Habermas
Understanding Jesus, Alister McGrath
Evidence That Demands a Verdict, Josh McDowell

If ever the Divine appeared on earth, it was in the Person of Christ. The human mind, no matter how far it may advance in every other department, will never transcend the height and moral culture of Christianity as it shines and glows in the Gospels.
■ Goethe

What If Jesus Had Never Lived?

Many years ago, actor Jimmy Stewart starred in a movie which has become a Christmas classic: *It's a Wonderful Life*. Around Christmas time each year, you can see that movie played on station after station, time after time. It has become a parable for our time to help us realize that one life does count. Jimmy plays George Bailey, who lives in Bedford Falls, New York. The movie begins with young George's high hopes and great dreams. He wants to get out of that "dreary little town . . . shake the dust off his feet, and do something big and important."

As his life unfolds, however, circumstances do not progress as he imagined they would. He tries to help the people in his town, and is continually thwarted by a high-rolling, sneaky, and unscrupulous banker, Mr. Potter, who makes Ebenezer Scrooge look like a boy scout. Potter owns most of the town because of his low-down, snake-in-the-grass ways. George falls into such despair as his own business faces ruin that he decides to kill himself. So he walks down to the main bridge over the river in town on Christmas Eve and gets ready to jump in.

Just before George leaps, Clarence shows up. Clarence, an angel who has not yet earned his wings, is assigned to help George through this crisis, and if he is successful, he will get his wings. Clarence looks like a regular human being. In a stroke of bumbling genius, Clarence falls into the river just before George jumps, and instead of plunging in to drown himself, George dives in to save Clarence.

That crisis averted, Clarence takes George on a miraculous journey through the town of Bedford Falls the way it would have been if George had never lived. On this journey, people who were nice young men in reality were boozers and n'er-do-wells because they lacked

George's good influence on them. Moral young ladies were now floozies, flaunting their bodies to whoever would pay them attention. The local pharmacist became a drunk and panhandler. The unscrupulous banker had the town under his complete control, and was extorting exorbitant profits from the hapless citizens. Night clubs and beer joints dominated the downtown area which once housed wholesome businesses.

Through this clever celestial illusion, Clarence was able to convince George that his life was not a waste: He had counted for something, and life was worth living. That job done, Clarence turned things back into reality, and George went home, was reunited with his wife and family, and lived happily ever after.

It is an intriguing storyline, isn't it, to imagine what the world would be like if someone had never lived? What if you had never lived? What would the world be like? What if Plato, Socrates, or Julius Caesar had never lived? What if Martin Luther had never lived? What if George Washington, Benjamin Franklin or Thomas Jefferson had never lived? What if Abraham Lincoln, Albert Einstein or Martin Luther King Jr. had never lived? What would the world be like?

Most important, what would the world be like if Jesus had never lived—this person who has had a greater affect on the world than any other person who ever lived.

In this chapter we learn that:

1. Jesus has improved the quality of education, health care, and poverty relief all over the world.

2. Jesus has encouraged the protection of the individual wherever government has respected biblical principles.

3. The twentieth century has taught us that when a nation forgets God, *calamity* results.

A lot of speculation arises in trying to answer this question, and we cannot say with assurance what the world would be like if Jesus had never lived. But we can give some good ideas as to what kinds of differences might exist between our world today and a world in which He had never lived.

Before we get into the specifics, it is necessary to acknowledge that many dreadful things have been done in the name of Jesus in the last two thousand years which Jesus would have had nothing to do with. The Crusades, the Spanish Inquisition, burning people at the stake for teaching their children the Lord's prayer in English (as was done in England in the early 1500's), the Salem witch hunts in our own country's early days. Certainly many awful things were done under the name of missions when we converted nationals, not only to Christ, but also to our own culture. Even today, horrible things are going on in the name of Christianity. In Ireland, Protestants and Catholics are killing each other. In Eastern Europe, the Middle East, and some African countries, Muslims and Christians are killing each other. Add to all this the highly publicized fall of prominent televangelists and other religious leaders, including an avalanche of lesser known local pastors, and the shame only deepens. The final indignity is the carnal lifestyle practiced by many individual Christians in America. We have a situation that is far from perfect, and we must be honest enough to admit it.

Certainly, the church is not without its warts and even tumors. Because the church is made up of people, it will never be perfect until it congregates in heaven. However, Christianity must be judged on the whole of its impact on the world, not just the parts in which followers and supposed followers of Christ have violated Jesus' teaching, and embarrassed Him. It is as Paul wrote to the Christians in Rome, "The name of God is blasphemed among the Gentiles because of you" (Romans 2:24).

Having owned up to the sins of the church, it is fair to turn the coin to look at the good which Christ's coming has caused. The good far outweighs the bad. I am indebted for a good bit of the information in this chapter to Dr. D. James Kennedy, who has written a marvelous and well researched volume entitled, *What If Jesus Had Never Been Born?* He deals extensively with the subjects summarized in this chapter.

What Impact Has Jesus Had on Social Issues?

Jesus has improved the quality of education, health care, and poverty relief all over the world.

Education

Christianity is basically a religion of the written Word. The Bible is the primary source of information for those who follow Christ. "The word of God is living and powerful, and sharper than any two-edged sword," penned the author of the book of Hebrews (4:12). "All Scripture is inspired by God and is profitable for teaching, for reproof, for correction, for training in righteousness; that the man of God may be adequate, equipped for every good work," wrote Paul (2 Timothy 3:16–17 NASB). Therefore, a Christian must be able to read the Word if he is to gain maximum benefit from his pursuit of Christ, the Living Word. As a result, "from its beginning the religion of the Bible has gone hand in hand with teaching. . . . Christianity is par excellence a teaching religion, and the story of its growth is largely an educational one. . . . As Christianity spread, patterns of more formal education developed" (*The New International Dictionary of the Christian Church*, 330–331).

Many of the world's languages were first reduced to writing by Christian missionaries in Bible translation. Wycliffe Bible Translators, the main Bible translation group, working in Bible translation, has translated the Bible for multiplied millions of people over the last number of decades, and has the goal of completing it for another three hundred million people who still do not have their own language written. This is done for the primary purpose of spreading the gospel, but it has the secondary result of promoting worldwide literacy.

The first printing press capable of mass producing books was invented to print the Bible. One of the passions of the Reformers was to get a Bible into the hands of everyone who could read, and to teach as many people as possible to read it. Many of Europe's finest schools were established to advance Christianity in some way. In the United States, nearly every early college was started for the same purpose. At the entrance to Harvard is a stone which carries this inscription:

> After God had carried us safe to New England, and we had built our houses, provided necessities for our livelihood, reared convenient places for God's worship, and settled the civil government; one of the next things we longed for, and looked after was to advance learning, and perpetuate it to posterity; dreading to leave an illiterate ministry to the churches, when our present ministers shall lie in the dust.

Yale and Princeton were started with similar purposes. The Reverend John Witherspoon, the president of Princeton, once said, "Cursed be all learning that is contrary to the cross of

Christ." If his curse stuck, learning at Princeton is now cursed. Dartmouth was founded to train missionaries to reach the American Indians. The college of William and Mary was established that "the Christian faith might be propagated."

Many colleges have defected from their original purposes; nevertheless, Christianity has played a primary role in educating Europe, England, and the United States, as well as Third World countries through missionaries who have educated countless millions in underdeveloped places. Had Jesus never been born, it is difficult to say what would have happened, but it is not readily apparent what other force in history would have generated the commitment and resources necessary to achieve such an overwhelming task.

Health Care

In addition to being a driving force in education throughout the world, Christianity has been responsible for advancing health care worldwide. From the early centuries of Christianity, we see Christians being moved to do something for the sick and hurt. The oldest hospital in existence today is the Hotel Dieu (God) in Paris, established by St. Landry around A.D. 600.

Jesus has impacted education, health care, and poverty relief worldwide.

Before that, Fabiola, a disciple of St. Jerome, is credited with having built the first hospital in the western world in Rome, around A.D. 400. Today, in the United States, many hospitals are called Saint *this* hospital, or Saint *that* hospital, attesting to their religious origins. There are Catholic hospitals, Lutheran hospitals, Baptist hospitals, Presbyterian hospitals, and so on.

Florence Nightingale was a devout follower of Christ, and as a result from compassion rooted in her faith, she initiated the institution of modern nursing. The Red Cross is a cousin to the YMCA, the Young Men's Christian Association. Louis Pasteur, whose advances in medicine made revolutionary impact, devoutly followed Christ.

Absolute faith in God and in eternity, and a conviction that the power for good given to us in this world will be continued beyond it, were feelings which pervaded his whole life; the virtues of the Gospel had ever been present to him. When he died, he was holding on to his wife with one hand, and to a crucifix with the other (*The Life of Pasteur*, 462, 464).

Albert Schweitzer spent his life helping establish a hospital in remote Africa. Radio station HCJB in Quito, Ecuador, after broadcasting the gospel for many years was prevailed upon by the sheer need to start a hospital for the people who listened to

---

Why I need to know this

If I don't know this, I may fall victim to the revisionist accounts of secular humanists who blame Christianity for many evils in the world and credit it for little good. I will not understand, and therefore will not appreciate, the unprecedented impact which Christ has made, not just in fitting people for heaven, but for making them forces of good on earth. I may shrink back when Christianity is criticized or ridiculed, thinking that Christ has not made a significant impact on the world. I underestimate the calamity that results in society when biblical principles are forgotten. I need to know this so I will never be tempted, myself, to abandon biblical principles to live by.

---

their daily radio broadcasts. Orphanages have been established in Korea which provide for medical and educational needs of the homeless. And on and on the list could go.

In the early days of developing countries of Africa, Asia, some parts of Latin America, the Islands, and other such places, the building of schools, the providing of public health, and many other services which stem the tide of suffering and advance human potential were established by the Christian church.

The Disadvantaged

Jesus set the tone for our response to the disadvantaged in Matthew 25 when He said, "For I was hungry, and you gave Me something to eat; I was thirsty, and you gave Me drink; I was a stranger and you invited Me in; naked, and you clothed Me; I was sick, and you visited me; I was in prison, and you came to Me." Then the righteous asked when they had done those things, and Jesus responded that to the degree that they did it to "one of these brothers of Mine . . . you did it unto Me" (verses 35–40 NASB).

Therefore, the church must take seriously this ministry to the disadvantaged, and it has, historically. Before Christianity was well established in the world, widespread charity was little known. In England during the 1800's, George Mueller founded orphanages in England which gave health and education assistance to thousands of children. While many examples could be given of Christian aid to the disadvantaged in the United States, it is also quite enlightening to realize that the United States, a nation founded to a significant extent on Christian principles, has been the most generous nation in the history of the world. We have given multiplied billions of dollars to the disadvantaged all around the world. After World War I, we gave massive amounts of financial, medical, and technical aid to other countries. After World War II, if we had wanted to, we could have ruled the entire world. We were the only ones with a deliverable nuclear arsenal. We had defeated all our enemies, and we could have used the situation to rule Europe, Japan and Russia. Instead, we gave billions of dollars to these countries to rebuild themselves.

This money cannot be attributed to the church in America, but I believe it can be attributed to Christ, because, going back to the beginning, He is the one responsible for the fact that the United States had such charitable intentions toward other countries. The United States is often the first one to offer disaster relief to other nations who have been devastated by natural disasters and wars. In my own lifetime, I can remember millions, and perhaps billions, of dollars going to give food and water to starving masses in Africa, water and medical aid to victims of floods and typhoons in Southeast Asia, technical and medical aid to victims of earthquakes in the Soviet Union and Mexico. We are a generous nation, and my own strong opinion is because we still carry the vestiges of Christian values upon which this nation was founded.

What Impact Has Jesus Had on Government?

Jesus has encouraged the protection of the individual wherever government has respected biblical principles.

The establishment of benevolent governments and the promotion of equitable laws has been a legacy of Christianity for hundreds of years. The dignity of the individual is a basic benefit of Christianity to the making of laws. The *Magna Carta* in England, which advanced the rights of the individual, was rooted in Christian values. The Preamble to the United States Constitution states, "We hold these truths to be self evident; that all men are created equal; that they are endowed by their creator with certain unalienable rights; that among these are life, liberty, and the pursuit of happiness . . ." The right to life, liberty, and the pursuit of happiness are linked to man's Creator. While not stated in such terms until the latter part of the 1700's, this expression of human dignity is rooted in Jesus' teachings. Through them the master is exhorted to treat the slave as he would like to be treated, knowing that the Heavenly Father is master of them both.

Based on such values, Christians have been hard at work throughout the centuries trying to preserve the dignity of all men. Slavery was outlawed in England in 1807 under the considerable efforts of Christians such as Granville Sharp and William Wilberforce. In the United States, slavery was opposed by many Christians and Christian organizations. Those who seriously regard the truth of Scripture cannot help but hold to a form of government which deals rightly with its people, affording them the dignity which they have as beings created in the image of God. This does not mean, of course, that we do not punish criminals. Rather, because of the dignity and value of the innocent, the guilty must be punished. To hold seriously to Scripture is to hold seriously to humane government.

"Human rights" grew from biblical principles.

In New Testament teaching, all power exercised by humans is to be wielded altruistically. Whether government over citizen, church over member, master (employer) over slave (employee), husband over wife, parents over children (and children over pets, by extension), the one in authority gets his right to authority from God and is responsible to use that authority for the benefit of those under it. Any other use of authority departs from Scripture. God never gave anyone permission to do mischief.

What Has the Twentieth Century Taught Us?

The twentieth century has taught us that when a nation forgets God, calamity results.

In a speech given in 1994 at a conference at Coral Ridge Presbyterian Church, Ft. Lauderdale, Florida, Gary Bauer related the story of a teacher who wrote a letter to the *Los Angeles Times*. She had been a teacher approximately twenty years ago. When she came into class in the morning, she would say, "Good morning, class." And the class would reply in unison, "Good morning, Miss Jones." Then, she married and decided to leave teaching to raise her family. With her family grown, she again applied for and received a teaching position. She went into class on her first day and said, "Good morning, class." To her mind-numbing shock, instead of hearing in unison, "Good morning, Mrs. Smith," one youngster in the front row shouted, "Shut up, witch!" Unfortunately, the word was actually worse than "witch" but I won't offend you by using it in print. Her letter asked, "What happened to America between "Good morning, Miss Jones," and Shut up, witch!"

What a dramatic, historic question! What happened to America during that twenty-year time? Alexander Solzhenitsyn gave us the answer in his commencement address to Harvard in 1978, an address which ostracized him from the politically correct crowd in America from that day on. He said, "The problem with America is that men have forgotten God."

That, Mrs. Smith, is what happened to America between "Good morning, Miss Jones," and "Shut up, witch!" Yours is almost a laboratory case study of the difference Jesus makes and has made in the affairs of men. You were in a time warp. The dramatic change in America began to manifest itself just as you left school to raise your family. In 1964, the United States Supreme Court ruled that the Ten Commandments could no longer be displayed in school and that state-sponsored prayer could no longer be offered in school. That decision reflected the growing godlessness of America and has helped produce a class with a smart alec in the front row who lacks the basic marks of a civilized person.

Before this devastating cultural collapse, the main problems teachers had with students were chewing gum in class, running in the halls, being late to class, and talking during class. These have been replaced by teacher physical abuse, students carrying guns, drugs in the high school, gang violence, teen-age pregnancy, and a collapse of cooperation between school and home, so that grades and college scores have fallen into the basement. We are now graduating from high school students who cannot read, cannot write, and cannot compute basic math. They have neither the social skills to succeed in a job nor the moral skills to marry, raise a healthy family, and contribute positively to society.

Certainly, to say that this is the only picture of youth today would be a big mistake. But it is even a bigger mistake to conclude that the problem is anything but cataclysmic, and a problem about which something must be done if we have any significant hope for the future.

In New York City many years ago, there were forty-four murders a year. As of this writing, there are approximately forty-four murders a week. It used to be safe to walk the streets of nearly any major town, including Central Park in New York. Now, when the sun sets, the deadbolts click into place. We are terrified in our own homes. Drugs are eating alive an entire generation of young people, consuming first their souls and then their bodies. Sexual immorality and sexually transmitted diseases are epidemic. A decade ago, herpes, warts, and other sexually transmitted diseases were being touted as epidemic, destroying the lives of countless thousands in America. Now you hear nothing of them, because a greater giant, AIDS, towers so tall that it casts its shadow over everything else. AIDS is indeed a frightening specter as it begins to cross over from the homosexual and drug culture into the heterosexual non-drug culture in America. Where will it stop? Well, it will only stop at the door of those who do not have AIDS, and marry those who do not have AIDS, and remain sexually faithful to that partner for life. Fidelity and celibacy form the only barrier, assuming the blood supply for transfusions becomes and remains untainted. Yet, horrible as AIDS is, it did not make the herpes epidemic go away. It is still out there, even though you never hear of it anymore. You cannot take coals into your bosom and not be burned, says the book of Proverbs. As a nation, we have taken coals into our bosom, and we are being burned.

> **Calamity follows a nation that forgets God.**

A rudderless ship adrift on an ocean, driven by gale-force winds and under full sail, will soon capsize. As a nation, gale-force winds are propelling our ship of state at breath-taking speed, but we have not furled our sails. We have lost our moral compass and the rudder dangles uselessly. Sure calamity lies ahead unless corrections are made.

People forty years old or older are able to see the laboratory test case. We saw America with God and we see America without God. America with God was, by comparison, a wonderful place (although by no means perfect). America without God will become a haunted house from which we may never escape.

Even in the small town I live in, I see the difference. Many of the teachers in the school system trained at a local Christian college. Many of the workers and business people graduated from that college. Many people still go to church. After church on

Sunday morning, you cannot find an empty table at any restaurant in town. Even non-Christians still cling to the values of the past. There are problems here, of course. There are still sin and crime. Yet many people still do not lock their doors when they leave their homes. They don't lock their cars. Theft rarely occurs. The State Farm agent told me when we moved here that in twenty-two years of being in the insurance business here, he has processed only two claims for stolen cars, one for each decade. Fast food people and clerks in stores are courteous and very helpful. If a mechanic looks at your car and finds nothing wrong with it, he doesn't charge you anything.

I don't want to make it sound like Utopia. It isn't. But it's better than a lot of places. And the interesting thing is, this town exemplifies thousands of small, rural towns all across America. Often, the more isolated the town, the more it clings to moral values. The moral jungle common to so many cities has not yet flourished in such towns.

Having lived nearly half a century, I can see clearly the difference between America with God and America without God. America without God breaks your heart. Even those with no personal interest in Christianity ought, for their own interests, to promote Christianity because it makes society and culture more pleasant for them.

Recent Historical Examples

Let's take it a step further. Let's remove all Christian restraints and see what can happen. Let's look at Germany in World War II, Russia under Stalin, China under Mao, just to mention a few godless societies. Hitler is commonly thought of as one of the most ruthless persons in history. The first victims of the Holocaust were people deemed by the state to be insane and incurable. Then, Hitler started in on the Jews. Besides Jews, the only voices to protest were courageous Christians, so he began working on them. By the time World War II ended, he had killed six million Jews and between nine and ten million others, many of them Christians. What a monster Hitler was. Most people who believe in Hell would say that if Hell contained only one person, he would be Hitler.

However, if you are comparing numbers, Hitler is a small player compared to Stalin. As Stalin was grasping for power, he killed between forty and sixty million of his *own countrymen*, many of whom were Christians. He viewed the church as an enemy to his atheistic state, and attempted to liquidate the entire Christian population.

But you don't get to the top of the pile of horror and infamy until you get to Mao Tse Tung. It is estimated that Mao was responsible for the deaths of over seventy million of his countrymen. Some of these were killed in "purges" or in slave labor camps. Others starved to death as a result of the failure of collectivism. In the Great Cultural Revolution, Mao also attempted to eradicate the church, killing an estimated twenty-two million.

Add to those numbers the millions killed in the communist takeover of Cambodia, and the countless multitudes killed in Korea, Vietnam, Laos, Thailand, Cuba, Uganda, Eastern Europe, Africa, and other places, and you come up with an estimated 130 million people (James Kennedy, *What If Jesus Had Never Been Born?*, 236).

If we are to be thorough in our investigation into how the world would be different if Jesus had not been born, we must look at the issue of abortion. In the United States alone, over twenty-five million children are not alive today because their mothers aborted them. Numbers can get stale, so let me tell you that that is enough people, using a rough estimate, to equal the population of Seattle, Portland, San Francisco, San Diego, Phoenix, Denver, Dallas, Fort Worth, San Antonio, Kansas City, Minneapolis, St. Louis, New Orleans, Memphis, Nashville, Louisville, Indianapolis, Atlanta, Columbus, Orlando, Philadelphia, Boston, Washington, D.C., and Richmond. Think of erasing those cities off the map. That many lives have been lost in the United States to abortion. It is beyond belief! Abortion worldwide is estimated to have killed *one billion* people.

All these people have been killed because people turned their backs on God. This is not a difference Jesus made, but it is a difference Jesus would like to have made. Certainly, it helps us compare a world with Jesus to a world without Jesus.

What if Jesus had never been born? Godless shedding of human blood would almost certainly have been worse. The world would be less educated. It would be much crueler, with fewer hospitals, poverty relief programs, and orphanages. Slavery might well still be common. If Jesus had not lived, the United States would not have had the influence in the world it has.

We began this book using the little essay, "One Solitary Life."

It stated that "all the armies that every marched, all the navies that ever sailed, all the parliaments that ever sat, all the kings that ever reigned, put together, have not affected the life of man on earth as much as that one solitary life." When you first read it, it may have sounded like an overstatement. But when you consider the impact Jesus has had on the world, it is truly terrifying to think what the world would be like without Him.

Speed Bump!

Slow down to be sure you've gotten the main points of this chapter.

Question Answer

Q1. What impact has Jesus had on social issues?

A1. Jesus has *improved* the quality of education, health care, and poverty relief all over the world.

Q2. What impact has Jesus had on government?

A2. Jesus has encouraged the *protection* of the individual wherever government has respected biblical principles.

Q3. What has the twentieth century taught us?

A3. The twentieth century has taught us that when a nation forgets God, *calamity* results.

Fill In the Blank

Question Answer

Q1. What impact has Jesus had on social issues?

A1. Jesus has _____ the quality of education, health care, and poverty relief all over the world.

Q2. What impact has Jesus had on government?

A2. Jesus has encouraged the _____ of the individual wherever government has respected biblical principles.

Q3. What has the twentieth century taught us?

A3. The twentieth century has taught us that when a nation forgets God, _____ results.

For Further Thought and Discussion

1. In what areas other than the ones mentioned in this chapter has Jesus made an observable difference in history, culture, and society?

2. What violated biblical principles have gotten us into the most trouble in the United States?

3. What do you think are the most important issues facing the United States today, and what needs to be done about them? What role do you think you should play?

What If I Don't Believe?

1. If I don't believe the impact Jesus had on society, I have to explain away all the benevolent things that have been done in His name throughout the centuries.

2. I have to explain the impact which Jesus has had on governments, especially the United States government. So many of the founding fathers were Christians, and so much of the good which the United States has done, as well as the evil it has refrained from doing, is traced directly to the fact that the nation was founded on Christian principles.

3. I have to explain the fact that the dreadful evils the United States is facing can be traced back to the abandonment of Christ by leaders in our nation, and the removal of positive Christian influence in all governmental institutions. For example, the posting of the Ten Commandments and the forbidding of prayer in the early sixties were both a reflection of a rejection of God, and an encouragement for even more rapid rejection of God by succeeding generations.

For Further Study

1. Scripture
Several passages speak of Jesus' impact on society and government, as well as the result of turning your back on Him. They include:

- Matthew 22:21

- Matthew 25:31–46

- 1 Timothy 2:1–2

- 1 Peter 2:13–17

- Hebrews 2:1–4

If you wish further study, read these passages and consider how they contribute to your understanding of the subject of this chapter.

2. Books

Several other books are very helpful in studying further this subject. They are listed below in general order of difficulty. If I could only read one of these, I would read the first one:

What If Jesus Had Never Been Born? D. James Kennedy
The Body, Charles Colson
Discovering the Laws of Life, John Marks Templeton
God, Country and Notre Dame, Theodore Hesburgh
How Should We Then Live? Francis Schaeffer

Alexander, Caesar, Charlemagne, and I myself
have founded great empires. . . . But Jesus alone
founded His empire upon love, and to this very
day, millions would die for Him. Jesus Christ was
more than a man.
■ **Napoleon**

9

Why Believe Jesus Was God?

It is one thing to believe that Jesus of Nazareth was an historical figure; it is quite another to believe that He was God. It is impossible to deny with any credibility that He lived. Historical and archaeological references to Him date from mere years after His crucifixion, and no major historian doubts that He lived. But is it certain that He was God? Well, in the eyes of many, that is an entirely different question. Many people who believe He lived do not believe He was God. Rather, they believe He was a great moral teacher.

Why would they not say He was a great moral teacher? Look at the greatness of His teachings! "Do unto others as you would have others do unto you," He said. What a lofty and marvelous teaching! It is one of the most powerful sentences ever uttered by a human tongue. That sentence alone, if believed and followed by everyone, would stop all war, all crime, all deliberate violence, and all of man's inhumanity to man. It would eliminate the majority of suffering we see in the world today.

"Love your neighbor as yourself," He goes on (Matthew 22:39). But more than that. "Love your *enemies*, and pray for those who despitefully use you." "If anyone strikes you on one cheek, turn the other to him." "If anyone asks for your shirt, give him your coat also" (Matthew 5:44, 39, 40). On and on it goes, the noblest teaching ever uttered or ever heard. So why would we not say that He was a great moral teacher? Indeed He was!

However, we cannot say that He was merely a great moral teacher. He said too many other things to allow us to stop there. He also said He was God. He claimed to be able to forgive sins. He said that no one could get to heaven except through Him. He said He was coming again to judge evil in the world, and reign forever in heaven. He said that He would judge you and send you to hell unless you accepted Him. He said one outrageous thing after another which prevent us from saying that He was merely a great moral teacher. If Jesus was not also God, then the one thing certain about Him is that He was *not* a great moral teacher. C.S. Lewis, a devoted Christian and scholar at Oxford, once wrote:

> I am trying here to prevent anyone saying the really foolish thing that people often say about [Jesus]: "I'm ready to accept Jesus as a great moral teacher, but I don't accept His claim to be God." That is the one thing we must not say. A man who said the sort of things Jesus said would not be a great moral teacher. He would either be a lunatic—on the level of man who says he is a poached egg—or else he would be the Devil of Hell. You must make your choice. Either this man was, and is, the Son of God: or else a madman or something worse. You can shut Him up for a fool, you can spit at Him and kill Him as a demon; or you can fall at His feet and call Him Lord and God. But let us not come with any patronizing nonsense about His being a great human teacher. He has not left that open to us. He did not intend to (*Mere Christianity*, 56).

As Josh McDowell writes in *Evidence that Demands a Verdict*,

> He was either a liar, or a lunatic, or the Lord. He said He was the Son of God, that He knew the future, that He was without sin, that He could forgive sins, and that people would go to heaven if they believed in Him and received Him as their personal savior. If those things aren't true, and He knew they weren't, He was a liar. If those thing weren't true, but He thought they were, He was a lunatic. Or, if those things were true, He is the Lord (104–107).

So, was Jesus a liar? It doesn't seem likely that a liar would be able to found his entire life on a lie, and yet be utterly blameless in everything else He ever said or did. Every word, every deed rang with high moral character. His mind was exceedingly clear at all times. He never lost the even balance of His inner being. He always returned the wisest and the most morally upright answer to those who were trying to trick Him or catch Him off-guard. He was consistently compassionate and cordial to His friends. He clearly and accurately predicted His death, burial, resurrection, the coming of the Holy Spirit, the establishment of His church, and the destruction of Jerusalem. He never once gained personally from His ministry, either in personal comfort, status, or wealth.

Lewis Sperry Chafer, the founder of Dallas Theological Seminary, said, "The Bible is not such a book as a man would write if he could, or could write if he would." The same is true of Jesus. No man who is a liar at the core of his being would invent Jesus if he could, or could if he would. Jesus' character is so far above the capacity of a man to imagine, before learning about Him, that He could not be logically considered an imaginative product of a lying heart. Someone who lived as Jesus lived, taught as Jesus taught, and died as Jesus died would not have been a liar.

In this chapter we learn three things concerning the deity of Christ:

1. Against all odds Jesus fulfilled all prophecies necessary to qualify as the Messiah.
2. Jesus' statements and claims exceeded the credibility of a human being, and could only be the words of God.
3. Jesus' deeds surpassed human ability, and could only be the works of God.

So, was He a lunatic? Just as Jesus' words and character show no signs of coming from a liar, they even less show signs of coming from a lunatic. Everything He did and everything He said had a sanity, a level-headedness, a ring of truth about it. If He were a lunatic, we would see some signs of it other than in His claims of divinity. His mind and character show no flaws. His logic and perception were beyond normal men's. No shred of evidence suggests He was not in His right mind. Only a person desperate for some reason not to believe in Him would call Him crazy.

Did Jesus Fulfill Prophecy?

Jesus, against all odds of chance, fulfilled all prophecies necessary to qualify as the Messiah.

If you let the evidence speak for itself, it seems unlikely that Jesus was a liar or a lunatic. So what is the evidence that He actually was God? Perhaps the most powerful place to begin is with fulfilled prophecy. A prophecy predicts the future. A great deal of prophecy permeates the Bible, especially the Old Testament. Jesus' birth and life were not random. He did not come helter skelter, any old way, and claim to be God. Rather, His birth, His life, and His death all conform to predictions written about Him hundreds and sometimes thousands of years before He was born. Let's look first of all at the prophecies He fulfilled.

Jesus fulfilled many Old Testament prophecies, some of them more obvious than others. For our purposes, we will focus on the more obvious ones. So that you can see them most clearly, I state the Old Testament prophecy briefly, and then its fulfillment in the New Testament. Let the record speak for itself.

1. *Prophecy: The Messiah would be born of a virgin.* "Therefore the Lord Himself will give you a sign: Behold a virgin will be with Child and bear a son, and she will call His name Immanuel" (Isaiah 7:14 NASB).

Fulfillment: Jesus was born of the virgin Mary. "She was found to be with child by the Holy Spirit. And Joseph . . . kept her a virgin until she gave birth to a Son; and he called His name Jesus" (Matthew. 1:18–25 NASB).

2. *Prophecy: The Messiah would be born into the family of King David.* "Behold the days are coming, declares the LORD, when I shall raise up for David a righteous Branch; and He will reign as king and act wisely and do justice and righ-teousness in the land" (Jeremiah 23:5 NASB).

Fulfillment: In the genealogy in the Gospel of Luke, Jesus is listed as being in the lineage of David. "Jesus . . . the son of David . . ." (Luke 3:23–31).

3. *Prophecy: The Messiah would be born in the city of Bethlehem.* "But as for you, Bethlehem . . . too little to be among the clans of Judah, from you One will go forth for Me to be ruler in Israel. His goings forth are from long ago, from the days of eternity" (Micah 5:2 NASB).

Fulfillment: Jesus was born in Bethlehem. "For unto you this day in the city of David (Bethlehem) there has been born to you a Savior, who is Christ the Lord" (Luke 2:11 NASB).

These prophecies have to do with the birth of Jesus, the Messiah. Other remarkable prophecies concern His death, some of them in the Old Testament, and some of the in the Gospels.

4. *Prophecy: The Messiah would be betrayed by a friend.* "Even my close friend, in whom I trusted, who ate my bread, has lifted up his heel against me" (Psalm 41:9 NASB).

Fulfillment: Jesus was betrayed by Judas Iscariot, one of His twelve disciples. ". . . Judas Iscariot, who also betrayed Him . . ." (Matthew 10:4).

5. *Prophecy: The Messiah would be tortured and crucified.* "But He was pierced through for our transgressions, He was bruised for our iniquities. The chastening for our well-being fell upon Him, and by His stripes, we are healed" (Isaiah 53:5 NASB).

Fulfillment: Jesus was beaten and then crucified. "Then he (Pilate) released Barabbas for them; but Jesus he scourged and delivered over to be crucified" (Matthew 27:26 NASB).

6. *Prophecy: Jesus would rise from the dead.* "For Thou wilt not abandon my soul to Sheol (the place of the departed dead); neither wilt Thou allow Thy Holy One to see decay" (Psalm 16:10 NASB).

Fulfillment: Jesus rose from the dead. "And the angel answered and said to the women, "Do not be afraid; for I know that you are looking for Jesus who has been crucified. He is not here, for He has risen, just as He said. Come, see the place where He was lying" (Matthew 28:5–6 NASB).

We could continue with many more prophecies and fulfillments. I have selected only a few of the major ones to give an idea of Jesus' remarkable life as it fulfilled one after another of the prophecies that told of the Messiah, in some cases, thousands of years before He was born. Again, in *Evidence that Demands a Verdict* (167), we see that the chance that any man might have lived down to the present time and fulfilled just eight of the major prophecies that Jesus fulfilled are 1 in 10 to the 17th power. That is, one in 100,000,000,000,000,000.

Jesus fulfilled all Messianic prophecies.

In order to help us comprehend these staggering odds, suppose we take this many silver dollars (10 to the 17th power) and lay them on the face of Texas. Now, as you know, Texas is a big state. If you could flip Texas west using El Paso as a hinge, Houston would land in the Pacific Ocean. If you could flip Texas east, using Houston as a hinge, El Paso would land in the Atlantic. If you could flip Texas north using the top of the panhandle as a hinge, the lowest part of Texas would land just short of the Canadian border. Texas is a big state. This many silver dollars (10 to the 17th power) would cover the entire state two feet deep in coins.

Now imagine that one of those silver dollars was painted red.

Blindfold a man and tell him that he can travel anywhere in the state he wants to, and pick up one silver dollar. Keep in mind that traveling at seventy miles per hour, he could not drive across Texas in a day. His chances of getting the marked silver dollar are approximately the same as a person fulfilling eight major prophecies of the Messiah by chance. Now, consider that Jesus fulfilled forty-eight prophecies. The odds that any one man fulfilled all forty-eight by chance are 10 to the 157th power. There is no practical way even to illustrate that number. Let's just say that there is about as good a chance of a tornado going through a junk yard and assembling a perfect automobile. When we look at the fulfilled prophecies in the life of Christ, the Bible becomes a very convincing book, and Jesus becomes a very convincing Messiah, God the Son.

Are Jesus' Words the Words of God?

Jesus' statements and claims exceeded the credibility of a human being, and could only be the words of God.

Admittedly, some of the things Jesus said were startling.

1. Jesus Claimed to be God

Some people assert that Jesus never claimed to be God. These people, whoever, are mistaken. I will give you the evidence and let you decide.

The name God gives Himself in the Old Testament is "I AM." An unusual name, it apparently refers to His eternality and self-existence. This means He was not created by anyone or thing as all other beings are, and He has always existed. It was a name so sacred that the Jews would not even utter it. In fact, they called their God by another name just so they wouldn't slip and call Him by His sacred name.

When God called Moses to lead the Israelites out of slavery in Egypt, Moses said,

Behold, I am going to the sons of Israel, and I shall say to them "The God of your fathers has sent me to you." Now they may say to me, "What is His name?" What shall I say to them? And God said to Moses to tell them that I AM has sent me to you. (Exodus 3:13–14 NASB).

Why I need to know this

If I don't know and understand that Jesus was God, I have no understanding of what true Christianity is all about. I am out of touch with the message of the New Testament and the teachings of Christ. If I don't know that Jesus was God, I am not yet a Christian, my sins have not yet been forgiven, and I have no assurance of life after death.

With this background, we understand more clearly the eruption Jesus caused among a group of Jewish leaders about His identity, when He said that Abraham rejoiced to see Jesus' day. "You are not yet fifty years old, and have You seen Abraham?" they challenged. Jesus said to them, "Truly, truly, I say to you, before Abraham was born, I AM."

You talk about mad! The steamed up Jewish leaders snatched up stones to throw at Him (John 8:52–59). Now, why in the world did they get so upset about Jesus' statement? True, there was never any love lost between the religious leaders and Jesus, and their conversation up to this point was anything but cordial. But when Jesus said, "I AM," they lost it. Can you imagine getting so angry at someone that you were willing to pick up stones and kill Him? But the reason was clear. There was no ambiguity whatsoever in the Jews' minds. Jesus, in their mind, had just blasphemed by claiming to be God. When Jesus said, "I AM," He claimed to be the same person who told Moses that He was I AM. And, what is the penalty in the Mosaic Law for blasphemy? Stoning! It is all perfectly logical when it is understood.

In another incident Jesus had been arrested in the Garden of Gethsemane and taken to Caiaphas, the high priest of Israel. They were interrogating Him, even knowingly accepting false witnesses **Jesus' words were the words of God.** against Him, in order to find some reason to put Him to death. The religious leaders had *had* it with Jesus, and were determined to get rid of Him once and for all. He had undermined their authority, their reputation and their credibility for the last time! After hearing all the conflicting accusations against Him, the high priest stood up and said,

"I adjure You by the living God, that You tell us whether You are the Christ [the Messiah], the Son of God." [Notice that the high priest equated being the Messiah with being the Son of God, so when Jesus called Himself the Son of God, He was admitting to being the Messiah, who is divine.] Jesus replied, "You have said it yourself; nevertheless I tell you, hereafter you shall see the Son of Man sitting at the right hand of power, and coming on the clouds of heaven." Then the high priest tore his robes, saying, "He has blasphemed! What further need do we have of witnesses? Behold, you have now heard the blasphemy; what do you think?" They answered and said, "He is deserving of death!" (Matthew 26:63–66 NASB)

This entire incident makes no sense whatsoever unless *we* understand that both Jesus and the religious leaders understood that Jesus was claiming to be God. The terminology is all correct. And the high priest accused Him of blasphemy for claiming to be God, and the penalty for blasphemy is death by stoning. Make no mistake. Jesus and the Jews understood that Jesus claimed to be God.

Michael Green quotes a rabbi who wrote about A.D. 160:

God saw that a man, son of a woman, was to come forward in the future, who would attempt to make himself God and to lead the whole world astray. And if he says he is God he is a liar. And he will lead men astray, and say that he will depart and will return at the end of days. (60)

The rabbi, Eliezer, was referring to Jesus, and Rabbi Eliezer unmistakenly referred to Jesus as God—a claim that Rabbi Eliezer was not sympathetic toward. But it indicates that Jesus did, in fact, claim to be God.

Another rabbi wrote in a similar vein. Rabbi Abbahu of Caesarea writes about a hundred years later than Rabbi Eliezer, but is quoting from a much earlier source:

If a man says "I am God," he is a liar; "I am the Son of man" his end will be such that he will regret it; "I shall ascend into heaven," will it not be that he spoke and will not perform it? (Green, 60)

Even Jesus' enemies verify that Jesus claimed to be God.

2. Jesus Claimed Things that Only God Can Do

God alone is the redeemer: "And He will redeem Israel from all his iniquities," we read in Psalm 130:8. But Jesus comes along and claims to forgive sin and give salvation (Matthew 9:2, Luke

7:50), things only God can do. In Matthew 9, some people brought a paralyzed man to Jesus.

Jesus seeing their faith said to the paralytic "Take courage, My son, your sins are forgiven." And behold, some of the scribes said to themselves, "This fellow blasphemes." And Jesus, knowing their thoughts said, "Why are you thinking evil in your hearts? For which is easier, to say, 'Your sins are forgiven you', or 'Rise, and walk?' " [Obviously, it is easier to say your sins are forgiven you, because who would know if it were actually true?] "But, in order that you may know that the Son of Man has authority on earth to forgive sins" then He said to the paralytic, "Rise, take up your bed, and go home" (verses 2–6 NASB).

Luke records a similar incident. Jesus is eating in the home of Simon the Pharisee, when a "woman of the world" entered weeping, and anointed Jesus' feet with perfume. The Pharisees were revolted. *"If He only knew what kind of person this woman is, He wouldn't let her touch Him,"* they thought. Jesus knew what Simon was thinking and asked him who would be the more grateful, someone who had been forgiven a little debt, or someone who had been forgiven a great debt. Simon replied, "I suppose the one who was forgiven more." Jesus answered that Simon had judged correctly, and linked his answer to the woman, observing that she had been forgiven much, and was, therefore, extremely grateful. Then He said to her, "Your sins have been forgiven." Those who were reclining at the table with Him began to murmur, "Who is this man who even forgives sins?" And He said to the woman, "Your faith has saved you; go in peace." Only if Jesus were God could He offer salvation to another.

3. Jesus Promised Things that Only God Can Promise

Jesus' promises are so extreme that He must be either God or deranged. His promises included not only this world, but also the world to come. He promised to give his believers abundant life here and eternal life there.

Concerning this life, He promised that God so loved the world that whoever believed in Him would not perish but have eternal life (John 3:16). He promised that He would give His life as a ransom for us (Mark 10:45). He promised that heaven and earth would pass away, but that His word would never pass away (Matthew 24:35). He promised that when He left earth to return to heaven after His crucifixion and resurrection, He would send the Holy Spirit to come and live within the hearts of believers to convict them of sin, give them a longing for righteousness, guide them into righteous behavior, and strengthen them to do God's will. He promised that He would ascend into heaven and sit down at the right hand of God the Father.

At one time earlier in my Christian life I questioned my salvation. I can't recall why I doubted, but it had very unpleasant side effects. A terrible fear of death gripped me. I developed a fear of flying. I was flying a lot then, perhaps 100,000 air miles a year; my livelihood depended on my getting on the plane every week. Turbulence would cause my heart to hammer my sternum in an attempt to break out of my chest until it was over or we landed.

I scoured the Scriptures to get relief. Two of His promises convinced me. First, He said, "the one who comes to Me I will certainly not cast out" (John 6:37).

Well, I had come to Him with all my heart and even begged Him to save me, to forgive my sins, and to give me eternal life.

Jesus' promises are . . . the promises of God

Hope began to stir in me. Then my readings took me to John 3:36, "He who believes in the Son [which I certainly did] has everlasting life." Well! That was all that could be said! Either I was a Christian and "safe" or else the Bible was not true and God was a liar. That couldn't be true. So all I had to do was accept it. I did and it helped tremendously.

These, of course, are not the only promises Jesus made about the world to come. He promised that He would give those who followed Him eternal life, that they would never perish, and that nobody would be able to snatch them from His hand (John 10:27–29). He promised that He would come again to close out history (life on earth as we know it), and He would judge the world for sin and righteousness. He used the figure of speech of separating the sheep from the goats (you want to be a sheep) (Matthew 25:31–33). That promise brings deep comfort to those who accept Him as Lord of their lives, and terror to those who haven't.

Are these the words of a man? Think about it. Who is the greatest man who ever lived? Plato? Socrates? Caesar? Alexander the Great? Napoleon? Thomas Jefferson? George Washington? Abraham Lincoln? Ghandi? Think about it. Anything any one of them has said falls so far short of what Jesus said that it is worse than comparing a monkey to Einstein. Their words fall far short of the character and tone and authority of Jesus' words. Jesus' promises are not the promises of a man. They are the promises of God.

Are Jesus' Acts the Acts of God?

Jesus' deeds surpassed human ability, and only could be the works of God.

We move now from the words of Jesus to the deeds of Jesus. We will look at this more closely in another chapter, but the most obvious deeds of Jesus which point toward His being God are His miracles. Whom do you know who can perform miracles? Each of His miracles proclaimed His divinity. John the Baptist wrote a letter and asked if Jesus was the one who was to come (meaning the Messiah) or was there another. Jesus' reply was,

> Go and report to John the things which you hear and see: the blind receive sight and the lame walk, the lepers are cleansed and the deaf hear, and the dead are raised up and the poor have the Gospel preached to them. And blessed is he who keeps from stumbling over Me (Matthew 11:4–6 NASB).

Miracles are not the only deeds which mark Jesus as more than a mere man. Perhaps the second most convincing act is that He accepted the worship of men. What kind of evil, what kind of delusion, what kind of warp would have to lie in the soul of one who would accept the worship of others if he were not God? Peter and some of the disciples had fished all night without result. As they rowed toward shore, they saw Jesus standing near where they would land. Before they reached Him, Jesus called out to them, "Let your nets down again, on the right side of the boat." It is hard to imagine how they reacted to this suggestion. With anger? With frustration? "Who does he think he is? We are the fishermen. He isn't. We've been out all night, fishing these waters from east to west, north to south, and here, where there would normally be no fish, He wants us to put our nets out again." It might have been ready obedience, though I vote for that response after anger and frustration. Nevertheless, they put their nets out on the right side of the boat, and nearly sank the boat with their catch.

Because we have not spent our lives fishing on the Sea of

Galilee, we might be tempted to pass over this as one of life's co-incidences. But these men knew how truly astonishing this was. In awe, Peter fell down and worshipped Jesus because he believed this to be a miracle, and that revealed Jesus as divine. Then a second astonishing thing happened. Jesus accepted Peter's worship.

Other places in the Bible record people falling down to worship other men or angels, and neither the angels nor the men would accept the worship. How could they? But Jesus accepted it calmly. It was right.

After Jesus had been crucified and resurrected, He appeared to His disciples hiding in an upper room, cowering in fear of the Roman authorities. If the Romans had crucified Jesus, what might they do to His closest followers? One of the disciples, however, was not there: Thomas. He was "from Missouri." He doubted the other disciples' report. He said, "Unless I see in His hands the print of the nails, and put my finger into the print of the nails, and put my hand into His side, I will not believe" (John 20:25). Hard core unbelief!

Eight days later, the disciples were all together again, with the doors shut, and suddenly in the middle of them stood Jesus. He said to Thomas, "Reach your finger here, and look at My hands; and reach your hand here, and put it into My side. Do not be unbelieving, but believing."

What a kind gesture! Jesus didn't say, "Thomas, you blockhead. What is it going to take to get through to you?" He didn't sigh, tap his foot, fold his arms in disgust, and say, "Okay, look. These are the wounds. Now are you satisfied?" Not at all. Instead, very gently, Jesus said, in essence, "Touch my wounds, Thomas, and believe. I love you. I want you as my disciple. Touch the wounds and believe."

Only God could do the acts Jesus did.

There is no indication that Thomas touched His wounds. Just the presence of Jesus and His gentle invitation were enough. Thomas might have dropped to his knees, or bowed his head, but the words that burst from his lips were, "My Lord and my God!"

Jesus didn't reply, "Oh, no, no, no! Don't say that." Instead, He said, "Because you have seen Me, have you believed? Blessed are they who did not see, and yet believed." Jesus accepted his worship.

In the Jewish culture where to recognize any other god (Commandment #1: Thou shalt have no other gods before me!) was blasphemy, no serious Jew would give a thought to worshipping anyone except the one they believed to be God. Jesus was God, so He naturally accepted the worship of those whom He had created.

Think, now. Are those the deeds of man? Think of the greatest man you have ever known of. Has anyone done anything to come within a hundred miles of Jesus? Alexander the Great? Plato? Socrates? Ghandi? George Washington? Abraham Lincoln? Think about it. Anything any one of them has done falls so far short of what Jesus did that it is worse than comparing a boxing kangaroo to a neurosurgeon. Their deeds fall so short of the actions of Jesus, they don't fit in the same category. These are not the deeds of a man, but of God. Jesus was not a man. He was God.

Conclusion

Why believe that Jesus was God? Because of the staggering prophecies He fulfilled, because of the character of His words, and because of the character of His deeds. Napoleon is reputed to have said,

I marvel that whereas the ambitious dreams of myself, Caesar, Alexander, should have vanished into thin air, a Judean peasant, Jesus, should be able to stretch His hands across the destinies of men and nations.

I know men; and I tell you that Jesus Christ is no mere man. Between him and every other person in the world there is no possible term of comparison. Alexander, Caesar, Charlemagne, and I myself have founded empires; but upon what do these creations of our genius depend? Upon force. Jesus alone founded his empire upon love; and to this very day millions would die for him.

Speed Bump!

Slow down long enough to be sure you've gotten the main points of this chapter.

Question Answer

Q1. Did Jesus fulfill prophecy?

A1. Against all odds, Jesus *fulfilled* all prophecies necessary to qualify as the Messiah.

Q2. Are Jesus' words the words of God?

A2. Jesus' *statements* and claims exceeded the credibility of a human being, and could only be the words of God.

Q3. Are Jesus' acts the acts of God?

A3. Jesus' *deeds* surpassed human ability, and could only be the works of God.

Fill In the Blank

Question
Answer

Q1. Did Jesus fulfill prophecy?

A1. Against all odds, Jesus _____ all prophecies necessary to qualify as the Messiah.

Q2. Are Jesus' words the words of God?

A2. Jesus' _____ and claims exceeded the credibility of a human being, and could only be the words of God.

Q3. Are Jesus' acts the acts of God?

A3. Jesus' _____ surpassed human ability, and could only be the works of God.

For Further Thought and Discussion

1. Why do you think most people consider Jesus to be merely a great moral teacher even though, if that were true, many of the things He said would have to either be lies or lunacy?

2. Some people claim that Jesus manipulated circumstances in His life so that He came out looking like He fulfilled Messianic prophecies even though He was not the Messiah. What is your reaction to that?

3. Do you think there is a relationship between many of the miracles Jesus did and the things He was saying? If so, what do you think the relationship is?

What If I Don't Believe?

1. If Jesus is not God, I must admit that the Bible is full of lies.

2. Jesus is not the savior of mankind, He cannot forgive sins, and I have no way of dealing with sins.

3. Someone might say that if Jesus is not God, I have no sins, and that would be true. But my sense of guilt and shame over things done wrong would still trouble me.

4. I have no hope of life after death, and no assurance of guidance in this life.

5. There is no such thing as right and wrong, and morally, I can do whatever society will let me get away with. On the other hand, others can do to me whatever society will let them get away with. The law of the jungle prevails: the survival of the fittest or the luckiest.

For Further Study

1. Scripture
Several Scriptures speak of the deity of Christ. They include:

- Mark 2:28

- John 1:1–14

- John 8:58

- John 20:28

- Philippians 2:9–11

Read these passages and consider how they contribute to your understanding of humanity's need for God.

2. Books
Several other books are very helpful in studying this subject further. They are listed below in general order of difficulty. If I could only read one of these, I would read the first one:

> *Know Why You Believe*, Paul Little
> *Essential Truths of the Christian Faith*, R.C. Sproul
> *Who Is This Jesus?* Michael Green
> *The Words and Works of Jesus Christ*, J. Dwight Pentecost

*Our Lord has written the promise of resurrection,
not in books alone, but in every leaf of springtime.*
■ Martin Luther

Was The Resurrection True?

Imagine you and a friend are in an inflatable rubber dinghy, lost for days on the ocean. The sail boat in which you had been sailing capsized and sank in a terrible storm. Loss of life and mind-bending emotional torment underscore your hunger and dehydration. A relentless sun broils you, and prowling sharks circle your fragile craft. Ships passed without seeing you. Days passed with no hope. Nights passed with no relief. How you have survived this long is a mystery even to you, but you both know that rescue must come soon. You cannot hold out much longer.

The daily routine is to sleep as much as possible to conserve energy. From time to time, you must clean out your dinghy, so today, when you awake, you flip the dinghy to wash it out. The sharks are gone for now. Other game fish are in the area. You are both exhausted, and turning the dinghy upright again exhausts you, and crawling on board again seems almost impossible. Your friend helps you get in, and then you try to help him. He no longer has the strength to help himself, so you tug as hard as you can, grab his soaked, tattered Levis and pull him. He flops like a tuna fish into the bottom of the dinghy. Seeing him like this takes something out of you. You wonder if you're going to make it.

In desperation you scan the horizon for the thousandth time. You spot a dot on the horizon. It is a ship. But you don't even bother to get excited any more. So many of them have sailed by, close enough for you to see them, but too far away for them to notice you. But this ship looms larger and larger. You can't believe it. Its wake tips the dinghy. You jump up and down and shout frantically, waving your arms. The ship passes. How could they not have seen you? They were so close they could have seen the red veins in your eyes. You slump to the floor, head dangling uselessly on your chest.

At least you know you are in the shipping lanes. But will another one come by in time? And how close must one come before it sees you? Hopelessness perches on your shoulder like a vulture on a carcass. But then slowly, oh, so slowly, the ship seems to be changing course. Is this simply an adjustment in their normal course to their distant destination? Is the ship still turning? Are you wrong? Can you see some writing on the side? No, you are not wrong. The ship is turning. You can't believe it. Had someone seen you after all?

You try not to hope, but, oh, dear God in heaven, the ship is coming back. It is coming back! As it nears, you see men over the deck rails. They throw you two life lines and pull them past your boat. You both topple into the water and grab the life ring. Momentarily, you are yanked under water, but then you surface again. A hoist hauls you up the side of the boat. Rough, strong hands pull you aboard. Choking with salt water and gasping from exhaustion, you collapse on deck while a circle of wide-eyed faces surround you. They jabber something you don't understand, but you don't mind. You are safe.

This story, as I have told it, has never happened on the one hand, and yet has happened many times over on the other. I have read many stories which contain similar features. Someone lost at sea has no hope. Then from somewhere that could not be predicted, help comes, and they are saved.

When I read stories like this, I identify so closely with the people in it that my muscles tense up, my heart beats faster, and when the shipwrecked get saved, I cry like a baby. I know they are going to be rescued, or else the story wouldn't have been written. No story like this ever ends, "And they died out there on that dinghy. No one ever saw them again." The absolute giveaway is that the story is always written in the first person, so the story couldn't be told unless the one telling it survived. I cry anyway. Certainly, many people have suffered more than I, but I have suffered enough that stories like this become very real to me. When one has experienced some pain, it is easier to identify with someone else's suffering. When one has been delivered, it is easier to put himself in the place of someone else's deliverance. As a result, the conflict is more enthralling, and the resolution more gratifying.

> **Jesus is our ship; the resurrection is our lifeline.**

Stories like this all end up with the people in deep trouble. You scan the horizon of their lives and no help appears from any direction.

They are without hope. Then, from somewhere unforeseen, hope appears, and finally they are rescued.

That is the significance of the resurrection! Mankind is lost and without hope. He scans his horizon in every direction, and there no help comes. Then, a small dot on the horizon grows larger and larger. Is it a ship? Yes, it is a ship. Does it see us? Yes, it sees us. It pulls up along side and throws us a lifeline. We can be saved if we'll just grab it.

In this analogy, Jesus is the ship; the resurrection is the lifeline. Without the resurrection, there would be no hope in life. With the resurrection, there is every hope. The importance of the resurrection cannot be overstated. Without it, we are eternally lost. With it, we can be eternally saved. Without it, Jesus is a liar. With it, His words can be trusted. Without it, we are adrift on the ocean of life, alone and without hope. With it, we can cling to the promises of God. It is dramatic beyond words, but that simple.

In this chapter we learn that:

1. The declaration of Scripture, the description of the crucifixion, and the testimony of history all agree that Jesus died.
2. These also agree that Jesus' tomb was empty.
3. The empty tomb can be explained with any credibility only by saying that Jesus rose from the dead.
4. The case for the resurrection is overwhelming if you accept evidence at face value, as you would for any other historical event.

On the resurrection of Jesus pivots the history of the world. The apostle Paul said, "And if Christ has not been raised, your faith is futile; you are still in your sins. Then those also who have fallen asleep in Christ are lost. If only for this life we have hope in Christ, we are to be pitied more than all men" (1 Corinthians 15:17–19 NASB). If Christ was raised from the dead, then everything He said can be trusted. If He didn't, nothing He said can be trusted. Everything stands or falls on the resurrection.

Therefore, we need to understand the resurrection as well as we can. By understanding it well, we can appreciate it. By appreciating it, we can experience more joy ourselves in being saved and be more inclined to share the good news with others. As we look at the resurrection, several important questions arise.

Did Jesus Die?

The declaration of Scripture, the description of the crucifixion, and the testimony of history all agree that Jesus died.

The Bible makes it perfectly clear that Jesus died. All gospel accounts and many references in the epistles state this unequivocally. The account of His crucifixion leaves no doubt about it. As we saw in a previous chapter, historical references outside the Bible indicate that Jesus was, indeed, crucified. He died.

Crucifixion was a particularly cruel form of execution. It is difficult to imagine any civilized government sanctioning such a barbaric form of execution. The person was either tied or nailed to a cross. If nailed, as Jesus was, the very thought of it brings a shudder. If tied to the cross, the immediate pain was less, but eventually in both cases, breathing became extremely difficult. As the body sagged, the pull of the arms upward made it impossible to exhale, so the person would push himself up with his legs to exhale and catch another breath. Exhaustion and pain made it impossible to sustain this position, and he relaxed his legs, making breathing difficult again. After this had gone on long enough, the executioners would break the legs of the victim. As a result, he would no longer be able to push up with his legs, and he would soon suffocate, being unable to breathe.

Jesus' death is irrefutable.

When Jesus' executioners came to break Jesus' legs, it was unnecessary because Jesus had already died. To be certain He had died, an executioner thrust a spear into Jesus' left side. The Bible says that out of the wound flowed water and blood. Medical doctors will verify this as a certain sign that death has taken place. The separation of blood from serum (water) is one of the strongest legal and medical proofs of death.

Hundreds, maybe thousands, of people witnessed that death. The executioner had to certify to Pilate that the prisoner was dead. If he was mistaken, his own life would be on the line. Nothing in the historical records suggests anything but that the prisoner was dead. Unless we are willing to trash the Bible and ignore historical evidence, we must conclude that Jesus died. It is fruitless to speculate on any other alternative.

Was the Tomb Empty?

The declaration of Scripture, the description of post-crucifixion events, and
the testimony of history all agree that Jesus' tomb was empty.

When Jesus' followers went to His tomb on the third day,
they found it empty. The Bible says that an earthquake occurred
and rolled the stone away from the tomb. The stone would have
been exceedingly heavy, weighing thousands of pounds. From
God's perspective, rolling the stone away from the mouth of the
tomb was not to let Jesus out, but to let others see He was gone.

The Jews and the Romans most definitely did not want that
to happen. Jesus had made it known that He would be killed, and
said that He would rise again on the third day. The greatest nightmare the Jews had was the need to prove that that did not happen. They wanted to prove that Jesus was just a man, not the
Messiah, and to put an end to His presence once and for all. The
nightmare was nearly as great for the Romans, because Jesus was
stirring up political unrest. Political zealots who wanted an
armed insurrection against the Roman government were hoping
that Jesus would lead the rebellion, though He never gave them
any reason to hope for that. Nevertheless, because of the expectations and hopes of others, Jesus was a thorn in the side of the
Romans.

> **Gospels:** the first four books of the New Testament, all of which tell the
> story of the life of Christ, though from different perspectives and for
> different reasons.
>
> **Epistles:** the remaining books of the New Testament which were letters
> written by Jesus' followers to several churches and individuals instructing
> them on various facets of the Christian faith and life.

For these reasons, the Jews demanded and received from Pilate a Roman guard outside the tomb for the period of three days.
In addition, a Roman seal was placed on the tomb, which meant
a death sentence to anyone breaking the seal. Nevertheless, on
Sunday morning after the crucifixion, Jesus' followers went to the
tomb and found it open. Jesus was gone, though His grave
clothes lay as though Jesus' body had evaporated from them. The
nightmare had come true for the Jews. Now they could not put to
death the rumor of Jesus being the Messiah. The nightmare had

come true for Rome, because it was terribly embarrassing for the sealed, guarded tomb of someone who said he would rise on the third day after his death to be found empty.

How Can the Empty Tomb Be Explained?

The empty tomb can be explained with any credibility only by saying that Jesus rose from the dead.

It is not surprising that critics of Christianity have zeroed in on the resurrection of Jesus Christ. If they can bring that down, they can bring everything down. But, as best-selling author Paul Little once said before he died, "After 2000 years, no one is going to ask a question that will bring Christianity crashing."

In fact, the attempt has backfired in a number of cases, with the skeptics coming to a personal faith in Jesus as a result of their study. The evidence for His resurrection from the dead was overwhelming. As we explained more fully in another chapter, attorney Frank Morison planned to write a book to show the error of the resurrection. However, his research compelled him to the opposite conclusion. Morison's book, *Who Moved the Stone?* powerfully argues the reality of the resurrection. Similarly, General Lew Wallace was researching the background for a historical novel about a Jewish contemporary of Christ.

The empty tomb can be explained only one way: Jesus rose.

After being overcome by the evidence for the resurrection, Wallace placed his faith in Christ and wrote *Ben Hur*, a riveting fictional story which supports the resurrection. As C. S. Lewis recounted in his autobiography, *Surprised by Joy*, the evidence for Christ's resurrection brought a reluctant Lewis, kicking and screaming, to faith in Christ.

If you apply the same tests to the resurrection as you would to any other historical event, you come away concluding that Jesus actually rose from the dead. Only those who do not want to believe it come to another conclusion, and must wrench the arm of historical research to do it.

There are three common attempts to explain away the resurrection.

1. The Theft Theory

The earliest attempt to explain away Christ's resurrection asserted that His body was stolen. Some way had to be found to explain the empty tomb, so the Jewish leaders bribed the Roman guards to report that Jesus' body had been stolen by His disciples while the soldiers had slept (Matthew 28:11–15).

This story was so clearly false that Matthew did not bother to refute it. As Paul Little observed: "What judge would listen to you if you said that while you were asleep your neighbor came into your house and stole your television set? Who knows what goes on while he's asleep? Testimony like this would be laughed out of any court" (*Know Why You Believe*, 52).

Why do I need to know this?

If I don't believe the resurrection is true, then Jesus cannot be God. He is just another human. The Bible cannot be trusted, and there is no hope for life after death, for divine guidance, or for truth or morality in this life. Human history pivots on the resurrection. If it is true, there is hope: if it is not true, then there is no reason to hope for meaningful earthly existence or life after death.

The testimony that Jesus' body was stolen, the very thing the Roman guard had been posted to prevent, was ridiculous for other reasons as well. How likely is it that *all* the Roman soldiers fell asleep when the ordinary punishment for sleeping while on duty was death? If they had fallen asleep, would none of them be awakened by the sound of the stone being rolled away from the mouth of the tomb? The heroic effort it would take to move a stone weighing thousands of pounds would alert soldiers placed right at the scene to guard the tomb, and threatened with their lives if anyone broke the seal.

In addition, the theft theory means that the disciples deliberately lied about the resurrection, gave their lives to spread the message, and ultimately died because of it. Would the disciples face torture and death for what they knew to be a lie? How likely would it be that none of the alleged conspirators would ever recant his story, even on his deathbed. Even if the disciples had stolen Jesus' body, how can we explain the post-resurrection sightings, including one by more than five hundred people at one time (1 Corinthians 15:6)?

As Professor E. F. Kevan summarized:

The enemies of Jesus had no motive for removing the body; the friends of Jesus had no power to do so. It would have been to the advantage of the authorities that the body should remain where it was; and the view that the disciples stole the body is impossible. The power that removed the body of the Savior from the tomb must therefore have been Divine. (*Evidence that Demands a Verdict*, 1:239)

2. The Swoon Theory

This theory asserts that Christ did not really die on the cross. Rather, Christ appeared to be dead but had only swooned from exhaustion, pain, and loss of blood. He revived when laid in the cool tomb. After leaving the tomb He appeared to His disciples, who mistakenly concluded He had risen from the dead. It's preposterous, but let's look at it anyway.

This theory first appeared at the end of the 18th century, which makes it a "Johnny-come-lately" in the extreme. None of the attacks made on Christianity in ancient times challenged the fact that Jesus died on the cross. As we said earlier, one of the responsibilities of the executioners was to make certain that Jesus had died. We are told that Jesus had already died before He was removed from the cross. However, to make doubly certain, one of the soldiers thrust a spear into His side, producing blood and water, a sure sign of death (John 19:33–34).

Jesus had suffered much even before He was nailed to the cross. He had undergone the horrible ordeal of a Roman scourging which shredded His back by a whip with pieces of glass and metal at the end of the leather strands. The governor's soldiers had struck Him on the head repeatedly. He had been forced to carry the cross from the governor's headquarters toward His place of execution until, due to Jesus' weakened state, another man was compelled to carry the cross the remainder of the way.

But suppose for a minute that the Roman executioners were wrong and Jesus had somehow survived and was buried alive. How likely would He have endured another thirty-six hours in a cold, damp tomb without food, water, or medical attention? Would He have survived being wound in heavy, spice-laden grave clothes weighing an estimated seventy pounds? Would He have had the strength to free Himself from the grave clothes, roll away the heavy stone sealing the mouth of the tomb, overpower the Roman guards, and then walk several miles on feet that had been mutilated with nails?

Even the now deceased German critic David Strauss, who did

not believe in the resurrection, recognized the absurdity of this theory. Strauss said:

> It is impossible that One who had just come forth from the grave half dead, who crept about weak and ill, who stood in the need of medical treatment, of bandaging, strengthening, and tender care, and who at last succumbed to suffering, could have ever given the disciples the impression that he was the Prince of Life. This lay at the bottom of their future ministry. Such a resuscitation could only have weakened the impression which he had made upon them in life and death—or at the most, could have given an elegiac [sorrowful] voice—but could by no possibility have changed their sorrow into enthusiasm or elevated their reverence into worship. (*Know Why You Believe*, 54)

One final objection to this theory should be noted. If Jesus had somehow recovered from a deathlike swoon, He would have been a liar. The Bible says that God cannot lie (Titus 1:2). Would a person of the integrity revealed in the Gospels have encouraged His followers to preach and base their lives on a lie? From beginning to end, the theory is shot through with the incredible. The only reason it received any credence whatsoever was that people were eager to have some way of explaining away the resurrection because they did not want to believe it.

3. The Hallucination Theory

According to this theory, the disciples so longed for their dead master that they imagined they saw Him and heard Him speak to them. Whether the disciples' experiences are called hallucinations, illusions, or visions, they are believed to be completely subjective, taking place only in the excited minds of the disciples.

This theory is unbelievable for several reasons. First, generally only very imaginative and nervous people hallucinate. Many people of varied dispositions, including hardheaded fishermen like Peter, claimed to see the resurrected Jesus.

Second, because hallucinations are highly subjective and individual, no two people have the same experience. But Christ appeared to groups as well as to individuals. For example, 1 Corinthians 15:6 reports an appearance to more than five hundred people at once, most of whom were still living at that time. How could five hundred people have the same hallucination?

Third, hallucinations typically occur only at particular times and places associated with the imagined events. However, Christ appeared in a variety of settings, such as: early morning to the women at the tomb (Matthew 28:9, 10); one afternoon to two disciples on the road to Emmaus (Luke 24:13–35); early one morning to His disciples by the Sea of Tiberias (John 21:1–23); and on a mountain in Galilee to more than five hundred believers (1 Corinthians 15:6).

Most importantly, as John R. W. Stott points out, hallucinations of this type always "happen as the climax to a period of exaggerated wishful thinking" (*Basic Christianity*, 55). However, the disciples were not optimistically looking for Jesus' resurrection. Instead, they disbelieved or doubted when they were told of His rising, and even when they themselves saw the risen Lord (Matthew 28:17; Mark 16:8, 11, 14; Luke 24:11–37; John 20:24–25).

Did the Resurrection Happen?

The case for the resurrection is overwhelming if you accept evidence at face value, which you would for any other historical event.

If you consider the evidence with an open mind rather than sift it through the grid of a predetermined conclusion, you will agree that the resurrection, as it is recorded in the Bible, actually happened. And the historical trustworthiness of the New Testament is confirmed by the three tests generally employed in the studies of history and literary criticism: the bibliographical, internal evidence, and external evidence tests.

The *bibliographic test* requires us, since we do not have the original documents, to reconstruct them well enough to see what they claimed Jesus said and did. The New Testament documents are *by far* the best attested from antiquity in terms of both the number of existing copies and the shortness of the time between the oldest copies and the original manuscripts. For example, shortly before his death Sir Frederic Kenyon, formerly director and principal librarian of the British Museum, concluded:

> The interval, then, between the dates of original composition and the earliest (existing) evidence becomes so small as to be in fact negligible, and the last foundation for any doubt that the Scriptures have come down to us substantially as they were written has now been removed. Both the authenticity and the general

integrity of the books of the New Testament may be regarded as finally established. (The Bible and Archaeology, 288–289)

The second test involves a consideration of the document's *internal evidence.* John Warwick Montgomery explains, "This means that one must listen to the claims of the document under analysis, and not assume fraud or error unless the author disqualifies himself by contradictions or known factual inaccuracies" (*History and Christianity,* 9). The New Testament authors frequently claim to have written as eyewitnesses or from firsthand knowledge (for example, Luke 1:1–3; John 19:35; and 2 Peter 1:16).

The test of *external evidence* seeks to determine whether other historical materials support or deny the internal testimony provided by the documents themselves. Careful examination of literature written at the same time as the Bible confirms the historical trustworthiness of the New Testament accounts. For example, after years of archeological and geographical investigation, Sir William M. Ramsay concluded that "Luke's history is unsurpassed in respect of its trustworthiness."

Multiple lines of evidence support the resurrection.

More recently, Oxford history professor A. N. Sherwin-White wrote of the Gospel of Luke's companion volume, Acts, that "any attempt to reject its basic historicity even in matters of detail must now appear absurd. Roman historians have long taken it for granted" (*Roman Society and Roman Law in the New Testament,* 189).

If the resurrection did not occur, how can one account for the transformation of Jesus' discouraged and defeated band of followers into dynamic, joyful people willing to suffer and die to preach a risen Savior? Why did none ever save themselves by recanting the story, or salve their conscience by a death-bed confession of the deception? How did this message gain so many adherents among people who had contact with the events spoken of and would have detected falsehood? (For example, in 1 Corinthians 15:6 Paul refers to more than five hundred people who saw the risen Jesus and were still living more than twenty years later).

Beethoven's great work is his *Fifth Symphony.* Shakespeare's great work is, perhaps, *MacBeth.* Michelangelo's great work is the Sistine Chapel. God's great work was Easter morning, when the God-Man who had been dead for three days was raised to life. It was His great work achieved, His great song sung. Everything rests on it. Everything. If the resurrection is not true, everything we believe and everything we hope for is a grand delusion or cruel hoax. Only a cynic, willing to apply one test of accuracy to all other historical events and a different test to the resurrection, discounts its actuality. For reasons of their own, people do not want to believe in the resurrection, and must, therefore, come up with whatever theory they can to explain it away.

Two hundred miles northeast of Los Angeles is a baked-out gorge called Death Valley—the lowest place in the United States, 276 feet below sea level. It is also the hottest place in the country, with an official recording of 134 degrees. Streams flow into Death Valley only to evaporate in the scorching heat, and a scant two and one half inches of rain falls on the barren wasteland each year.

But some years ago, an amazing thing happened. Due to a freak weather pattern, rain fell into the bone-dry earth for nineteen days straight. Suddenly, millions of seeds, which had lain dormant for untold years burst into bloom. The Valley of Death exploded into beauty, color, and life.

This is the message of the resurrection. Life springs forth from death. A desert becomes a garden. Beauty transcends the ugly. Love overcomes hatred. A tomb is emptied. The grim and haunting outline of a cross is swallowed in the glow of an Easter morning sunrise.

Speed Bump!

Slow down to be sure you've gotten the main points of this chapter.

Question
Answer

Q1. Did Jesus die?

A1. The declaration of Scripture, the description of the crucifixion, and the testimony of history all agree that Jesus *died*.

Q2. Was the tomb empty?

A2. The declaration of Scripture, the description of post-crucifixion events, and the testimony of history all agree that Jesus' tomb was *empty*.

Q3. How can the empty tomb be explained?

A3. The empty tomb can be explained with any credibility only by saying that Jesus *rose* from the dead.

Q4. Did the resurrection happen?

A4. The case for the resurrection is *overwhelming* if you accept evidence at face value, as you would for any other historical event.

Fill In the Blank

*Q*uestion *A*nswer

Q1. Did Jesus die?

A1. The declaration of Scripture, the description of the crucifixion, and the testimony of history all agree that Jesus _____.

Q2. Was the tomb empty?

A2. The declaration of Scripture, the description of post-crucifixion events, and the testimony of history all agree that Jesus' tomb was

_____.

Q3. How can the empty tomb be explained?

A3. The empty tomb can be explained with any credibility only by saying that Jesus _____ from the dead.

Q4. Did the resurrection happen?

A4. The case for the resurrection is _____ if you accept evidence at face value, as you would for any other historical event.

For Further Thought and Discussion

1. Why do you think people have such a difficult time accepting the resurrection?

2. If God were going to do something highly extraordinary for the benefit of mankind, would not the resurrection qualify as that truly extraordinary event? If the event God chose to do for mankind were a different kind of miraculous thing, do you think people would have such a difficult time accepting it?

3. Why do you thing God chose the act of resurrection, as opposed to something else, to be the pivotal event in history?

What If I Don't Believe?

1. If I don't believe the resurrection, I reject the very heart of Christianity. It is like trying to be an American, but rejecting the Declaration of Independence and Constitution. Those are the defining core of what it means to be "American."

2. I reject Christ if I reject the resurrection, because He stated that His entire purpose in coming to earth was to die for our sins, and be raised again to provide new life for us.

3. I reject the Bible, since rejecting the word of Christ and rejecting the Bible are the same thing.

For Further Study

1. Scripture
Several Scripture passages in the Bible speak of the resurrection of Christ. They include:

- Matthew 28:6

- Acts 17:31

- Romans 1:1–4

- 1 Corinthians 15:12–20

- Ephesians 1:18–23

If you wish further study, read these passages and consider how they contribute to your understanding of the importance of the resurrection.

2. Books
Several other books are very helpful in studying further this subject. They are listed below in general order of difficulty. If I could only read one of these, I would read the first one:

Know Why You Believe, Paul Little
The Resurrection Factor, Josh McDowell
Who Is This Jesus, Michael Green
Understanding Jesus, Alister McGrath
Evidence that Demands a Verdict, Josh McDowell

Philosopher David Hume in 1776 stated, "I see the twilight of Christianity." I'm afraid that David Hume couldn't tell the difference between a sunrise and a sunset.
■ **George Sweeting**

What Is Jesus Doing Now?

In Mark Twain's engaging book, *The Prince and the Pauper*, the prince of England, Edward Tudor, looked exactly like a London pauper, Tom Canty. Through a series of incredible coincidences, the identities of the prince and the pauper are reversed, so that everyone thinks that the pauper is the prince, and vice versa. Tom Canty lives in the palace and Edward Tudor lives on the streets, begging and using his wits to keep himself fed and alive. A sometimes hilarious and often poignant story unfolds for each person with his new identity.

The king of England, the father of Edward Tudor, was not a careful and just man. He ruled without understanding what the common man was going through, without realizing how noblemen preyed on the fortunes of the poor, and without understanding how many of the arbitrary laws caused untold hardship and suffering on the poor. The young prince (now a pauper), seeing life from the other side of the tracks, resolves that when he is king, he will rule more wisely and compassionately. But would he ever be king? When he tries to make others understand and believe who he is, they all laugh at him, and think he is mad. The more he tries to convince them that he is heir to the throne, the more insane they think he is. He goes hungry, ragged, filthy, and mocked. Other poor people spit on him, and the rich mistreat him. Nevertheless, he never stops acting like a prince. He never returns evil for evil, and tries to treat others with the dignity and respect they deserve.

When it looks as though he will never be returned to his rightful position as the prince of Wales, the next king of England, an equally incredible set of circumstances unfolds which restores to him his identity. His father dies, and he is placed on the throne of England as King

Edward VI. His experience has changed him dramatically, however. Having spent time among the "common folk," his whole perspective has shifted. He rules with more wisdom and compassion than he ever would have possessed before. He considers how the laws of England affect the poor and the common man, and makes every effort to be a truly good king.

What a good and wonderful thing it was that Edward was king. How fortunate for England. How helpful for the common man. Edward was now where he belonged, in a position to do good for his subjects. As the years progressed, Edward's wisdom, kindness, and benevolence unfolded for the welfare of England, and he exemplified the highest and noblest of what it meant to be king.

In this chapter we learn that:

1. Jesus is in *heaven* now, sitting at the right hand of God the Father.
2. Jesus is *praying* to the Father on behalf of His children, and is *preparing* heaven for our arrival.
3. Jesus is *building* His church on earth.

There are several interesting parallels between the story of Edward, prince of Wales who became king of England, and Jesus. Jesus left His original royal home and lived among the common man. While He was on earth, He tried to make people believe who He was, but most did not believe Him. They thought He was a madman or an impostor. They ridiculed Him, spat upon Him, beat Him, and finally killed Him. And when Jesus was restored to His royal estate, He was finally in a position to bestow all the wisdom, the kindness, and the benevolence that He possessed.

So far in our study of Jesus, we have looked at who Jesus was, what He taught, and what He did, and how He has affected history. We have looked at the significance of His death and resurrection. Now, we want to look at the very interesting subject of what He is doing now. Nearly two thousand years ago, Jesus returned to His rightful place in the throne room of heaven, where He is fulfilling the reign for which His time on earth prepared Him. But what is that? What is Jesus doing now? As we investigate that question, we will look at several important things.

Where Is Jesus Now?

Jesus is in heaven now, sitting at the right hand of God the Father.

One of the churches I pastored brought in a Christian illusionist as an outreach event into the community. It was very successful, and scores of people came to Christ while he was there. He was an amazing performer, careful to emphasize that everything he did was an illusion, a trick, and that there was no "magic" involved. In fact, he said that anyone in the room could do what he did if he practiced for twenty-five years. The most amazing thing he did was seemingly to levitate. I was sitting not twenty feet from him as he slowly began to rise from a pillow until he was suspended about six feet from the ground. Assistants passed metal hoops around him to show that there were no wires. I know how the church is constructed, so there could not be anything beneath him, or above him, such as magnets or so forth. Afterward I said to him, "That intrigued me. If I promise, cross my heart and hope to die that I will never tell a soul, will you tell me how you did that?" He said, "No." That was the end of that.

Why do I need to know this?

It is important for me to understand what Jesus is doing now so that I don't feel alone and helpless as I live, and so that I don't get the impression that things are out of control and God doesn't have a plan that He is working out. God does have a plan. He does have a purpose for this period in history, and God is watching over us during this time, looking out for our welfare. It might be easy to get discouraged if we did not understand what Jesus is doing now.

While people perform tricks to astound, Jesus always did the real thing. Jesus' resurrection was truly dramatic. Death, the final and ultimate enemy, is the one thing humanity is not able, nor ever will be able, to conquer. The yawning, black jaws of death which gape at the end of each person's life never allow any to escape. Jesus, however, was different. He escaped.

If a person could come back from the dead by his own power, he could do anything. If a person could predict that he would die and rise again, and then actually do it, anything else he said could be trusted. Yet the resurrection was by no means the only astonishing thing in Jesus' life. Perhaps the second most astonishing thing was His ascension into heaven.

Jesus appeared to His disciples a number of times after His resurrection over a period of forty days, giving them their final instructions concerning the kingdom of God. Then, one day, He gathered them together on the Mount of Olives, a large hill to the east of Jerusalem.

This was a very special time, the last time He would see His disciples until they got to heaven. Surely, what He had to say to them would be some of the most important things He would ever say. He told them to stay in Jerusalem until they were baptized with the Holy Spirit, and to take the message of salvation to the whole world. Then, as they listened to Him, His feet lifted off the ground. Slowly and gently He began to rise. Soon He

Jesus is in a position of authority in heaven.

was above their heads, above the trees, above the hill. Higher He floated, and higher. Then, at some height, we do not know how high, He touched a cloud, and He disappeared into it, just as an airplane does taking off from the airport on a cloudy day. You could see Him for a while, then His head disappeared into the cloud, then His body, His feet—and He was gone!

The Bible says,

> And as they were gazing intently into the sky while He was departing, behold, two men in white clothing stood beside them; and they also said, "Men of Galilee, why do you stand looking into the sky? This Jesus, who has been taken up from you into heaven, will come in just the same way as you have watched Him go" (Acts 1:10–11 NASB).

This seems pretty understated to me. I don't know for sure, but my guess is that if we said, "And as they were standing there, craning their necks, jaws slack, eyes bugging, weak-kneed, stoop-shouldered and short of breath" . . . it would probably be closer to the truth. It must have been a truly sensational event!

Where, then, did Jesus go? As we piece together scriptural references, we learn that He ascended into heaven, and sat down at the right hand of God the Father in the heavenly throne room. God

> raised Him from the dead, and seated Him at His right hand in the heavenly places, far above all rule and authority and power and dominion, and every name that is named, not only in this age, but also in the one to come (Ephesians 1:20–21).

From this we learn several things. First, Jesus is seated at the right hand of God, a place of supreme authority. It involves possessing the throne without dispossessing the Father. All the glory, authority, and power are shared by the Father with the Son.

There is something very wonderful and mysterious about Jesus, however, because, as a man, His body is in the throne room in heaven. We even see Him standing (presumably out of concern) in the throne room as Stephen, the first martyr of the church, is stoned in Acts chapter seven. As God, however, He is spiritually present everywhere. In fact, the Bible makes it clear that Jesus lives within every believer (Colossians 1:27). So Jesus embodies this wonderful wedding of the human and divine: the God-Man resides in the throne room in heaven bodily, yet is omnipresent spiritually (everywhere simultaneously), a characteristic He shares with God the Father and God the Holy Spirit.

Now that He is in heaven, Jesus has all authority, although the ultimate victory which He will experience over sin and death and hell is being withheld, not for lack of power, but because of the hidden purposes of God the Father. In Psalm 110:1 we read, "The Lord [God the Father] says to my Lord [Jesus]: Sit at my right hand, until I make Thine enemies a footstool for Thy feet" (NASB). First Peter 3:22 declares that angels, authorities and powers are subject to Jesus. We have already seen in Ephesians 1:20–22 that all things are "under His feet," meaning subject to Him. Yet, for reasons known to God, the ultimate victory is being withheld until the fullness of time is complete.

What Is Jesus Doing Now in Heaven?

Jesus is praying to the Father on behalf of His children, and is preparing heaven for our arrival.

The first thing Jesus did when He returned to heaven was to send the Holy Spirit to earth to indwell all believers in Him. Jesus was speaking with His disciples shortly before His crucifixion and told them about the coming of the Holy Spirit. "Nevertheless I tell you the truth. It is to your advantage that I go away; for if I do not go away, the Helper [Holy Spirit] will not come to you; but if I depart, I will send Him to you" (John 16:7). Then, on the Mount of Olives just before He ascended into heaven, Jesus said, "for John [the Baptist] truly baptized with water, but you shall be baptized with the Holy Spirit not many days from now" (Acts 1:5). The Holy Spirit, then, as we will see more completely in another volume in this series, indwells each believer, leading, guiding and empowering believers to pursue the will of God.

After that first act of Jesus after He returned to heaven, Jesus is ministering to us primarily in two ways.

1. In Heaven, Jesus Prays for Us

In Luke 22:31–32, Jesus is talking with His disciples just hours before He was to be arrested and crucified. They were discussing the coming kingdom and the role the disciples would play in it. Knowing that danger for them all lurked right around the corner, Jesus said to Peter, "Simon, Simon! Indeed, Satan has asked for you, that he may sift you as wheat. But I have prayed for you, that your faith should not fail; and when you have returned to Me, strengthen your brethren." Jesus prayed for Peter, and in Peter's hour of greatest need, Jesus' prayer for him was answered. That prayer ministry for us continues, now that Jesus is in the throne room of heaven. To whom is Jesus praying? To God the Father, of course.

In Hebrews 7:24–25, we read, "because He abides forever, [Jesus] holds His priesthood permanently. Hence, also, He is able to save forever those who draw near to God through Him, since He always lives to make intercession for them. (NASB). Jesus prayed for all believers also in John 17:21: "[I pray] that they may all be one; even as Thou, Father, art in Me, and I in Thee, that they also may be in Us; that the world may believe that Thou didst send Me." (NASB).

I doubt that Jesus is limited to praying only for us that we not sin and for us to have unity, but those would be among the things He prays for us, and the kind of things He prays for us. He also intercedes for us when we do sin. In 1 John 2:1–2, we read, "My little children, I am writing these things to you that you may not sin. And if anyone sins, we have an Advocate with the Father, Jesus Christ the righ-teous; and He Himself is the propitiation [satisfaction] for our sins; and not for ours only, but also for those of the whole world" (NASB).

Have you ever tried to stop sinning? I mean, have you ever made the decision that you would never sin again? I think most serious Christians have. But it will drive a person crazy because sin is not only what we do, it is what we do not do. Sin is not merely action, but also attitude and motive. A failure to love as Jesus loves is sin. A failure to forgive as Jesus forgives is sin. A failure to submit to others and serve them as Jesus does is sin. When we compare our actions with the actions of others around us, we may look bad or we may look good. But when we compare our attitudes and motives with Jesus' attitude and motives, we all

Jesus still ministers for us in heaven.

look pretty bad. When we realize it is hopeless for us to live as righteously as Jesus did, it becomes significant that Jesus is praying for us that we not sin, and that He is our advocate, our defense attorney when we do. When we sin, Satan accuses us before God day and night (Revelation 12:10). Jesus is our advocate. Satan screams, "Look at Max! Look at him. He is being selfish and unloving. His wife asked him a simple question, and he snapped at her. That's a SIN," he rails. Jesus stands before the court and says, "Yes, it is a sin. But Max believes in Me, and has received Me as his personal savior. Though imperfect, he has committed his life to following Me. I died for that sin. I paid his price." The Judge, God the Father, says, "The sin is forgiven. Case dismissed."

One of the sweetest words in all of life is that wonderful word "forgiven." Without it, the full force of our sin would come crushing down upon us like an avalanche of rocks on an unsuspecting hiker. With it, the rocks dissolve to shadows, and they pass over us harmlessly. Jesus sits beside God the Father in heaven praying for us, and coming to our defense when we sin. How can we ever thank Him?

2. In Heaven, Jesus Is Preparing a Place for Us

In John 14:1–3, we read,

Let not your heart be troubled; believe in God, believe also in Me. In My Father's house are many dwelling places; if it were not so, I would have told you; for I go to prepare a place for you. And if I go and prepare a place for you, I will come again, and receive you to Myself; that where I am, there you may be also (NASB).

If bad things in life do nothing else, they help us appreciate the good things. One Sunday, after preaching at the church I was pastoring in Austin, I flew to Oklahoma City and preached at an evening Bible conference, and returned to the airport to fly home. We taxied out to the runway but when we normally would have taken off, the plane whooshed a bit, but didn't go anywhere. We limped back to the gate and waited. Finally, we all got off the plane. I waited for a very long time at the gate counter. At last they rescheduled me for an 8:00 A.M. Monday flight. I received a voucher to stay at a local hotel. I got to the hotel quite late and I hadn't eaten dinner, and was starving. There was no restaurant and no newsstand at the hotel. A room and a bed. That was it.

I can't fly home tomorrow looking like I'll look, I thought. Spying a Texaco station down the road a ways, I figured I could buy a razor, shaving cream, tooth brush and paste, and comb there. But I didn't have enough cash—the automatic teller machine at the airport hadn't been working. I had three dollars. A hamburger shop was still open, and I was starving. Do I eat or shave? I could buy the hygiene stuff with a credit card. So I trudged down the road to the Texaco station, bought what I needed, and started back toward the restaurant (which was in the other direction from the hotel) to spend my three dollars. Then in what seemed like a symbolic rubbing of my nose in misfortune, it started to rain. Suddenly. Without warning.

I ducked into the restaurant, ordered a hamburger, and took it back to the hotel where I ate it while watching highlights of the day's baseball games. Within fifteen minutes, it felt like I had eaten a cannon ball. I started to feel a little sick. I tried to go to sleep, but it was too warm so I turned on the air conditioning. One of those wide, on-the-floor-under-the-window units, it made more noise than a bulldozer. And the bed was right next to it, so that arctic air blew right in my face. *I'm going to catch a cold,* I thought. So I pulled the mattress to the floor, out of the wind, but the floor space wasn't big enough for the mattress. So I hoisted the mattress back onto the bed. I laid down, read my Bible, prayed, and turned off the light. Then the hamburger exploded. I had to sit up, or else I felt sick. I sat up until 2:00 A.M. watching professional rodeo highlights on ESPN and finally drifted off to sleep.

I was supposed to get a wake up call at 6:00 A.M. The phone rang at 3:30 A.M.

"Mr. Anders, did you want to get up now? A group has to be at the airport by 4:30 A.M. and I didn't know if you were part of that group."

"No ma'am. If you could call me at 6:00 A.M."

"Very well, sorry to disturb you."

"Think nothing of it."

I got on the plane looking like a vagrant. Black circles ringed my eyes. My hair lay plastered flat and gummy in the back and frizzy on top from having been rained on. My suit was wrinkled and dimpled from the rain, my shoes muddied. I was wearing a two-day-old shirt, socks and underclothing. We landed in Dallas for my connection to Austin. I was sitting there, out of my mind with fatigue and disorientation, and sure enough:

"Well, hi, Max! What are you doing here?" A family from my church. They had had a good night's sleep the night before, had showered, dressed in fresh clothes, and eaten. I burst into an immediate explanation of why I looked the way I did, lest they think I was on a secret drinking binge. For a split second, I considered trying to talk with a New Jersey accent and convince them that I wasn't this guy named Max, that I was his double.

> From heaven, all life's pains will seem like no more than a bad night in a cheap hotel.

I tell this story to highlight two things. First, it means something that Jesus is preparing a place for us. The hotel had not "prepared a place for me." They had not provided adequately for some basic needs. Jesus does. Jesus will have everything ready that He wants for us. It will be a time of peace, of love, of joy, and of rejoicing. It will feel more like "home" than anyplace we have ever been before.

Second, this story is really a microcosm of life. Life is like my bad night in Oklahoma City. Things beyond your control go awry. You think you have figured things out, and they fall apart in your hands. When you try your hardest, you get rained on. But as Mother Teresa once said, when we get to heaven, all the problems and pain of this life will seem like no more than a bad night in a cheap hotel. And why? Because when we get to heaven, it will be prepared for us. Figuratively speaking, the planes will leave on time. The hotel will roll out a red carpet when you arrive. You will be able to be served in a restaurant or order room service. Whatever you like. There will be a newsstand open, so that you can get the toiletries you need. There will be no air-conditioning because the temperature is already perfect. Wake up calls will come at the right time. Breakfast will be served in bed, if you wish. Now, please don't let me miscommunicate. That is not what I think heaven is going to be like. I am using it as a metaphor. In heaven, everything will work, everything will go off on time. Everything will be as it should be. That is because Jesus is preparing now for our arrival.

While theology text books list more ministries which Christ has in heaven, this covers two of the most obvious ones.

What Is Jesus Doing Now on Earth?

Jesus is building His church.

After Jesus had spent considerable time ministering to the multitudes, He began to spend a greater amount of His time preparing His disciples for His eventual departure from earth. One day, after entering the district of Caesarea Philippi, Jesus asked His disciples,

"Who do people say that the Son of Man is?" And they said, "Some say John the Baptist; and others, Elijah; but still others, Jeremiah, or one of the prophets." He said to them, "But who do you say that I am?" And Simon Peter answered and said, "Thou art the Christ, the Son of the living God." And Jesus answered and said to him, "Blessed are you, Simon Barjona (son of John), because flesh and blood did not reveal this to you, but My Father who is in heaven. And I also say to you that you are Peter, and upon this rock I will build My church; and the gates of Hades shall not overpower it" (Matthew 16:13–18 NASB).

Just before He left earth, Jesus directed His followers to "go into all the world and preach the gospel to every creature" (Mark 16:15), and not to worry, because He would work with them and be with them, "even unto the end of the age" (Matthew 28:20). Christ is the cornerstone of this church, and individual Christians are "living stones" (1 Peter 2:5), "in whom the whole building, being fitted together is growing into a holy temple in the Lord; in whom you are also being built together into a dwelling of God in the Spirit" (Ephesians 2:21–22 NASB). As one believer tells another, and that person tells another, and he tells yet another, the church (the totality of all believers in Christ) is built, and Satan will never be able to stop it.

After seventy years of state-imposed atheism in Russia, a revival has exploded there like nothing that has ever been seen in church history. Satan couldn't stop the church. Mao Tse Tung tried desperately to stamp out the church in China in the 1960's and 70's. So did his successors. Now, such prohibitions are beginning to lift a little, and we are finding that the church in China numbers in the tens of millions, headed to the hundreds of millions. Satan couldn't stop the church. In the Eastern European countries which used to be part of the Soviet bloc before the Soviet Union disintegrated, ruthless dictators tried to stamp out the church.

Jesus is building His church.

Then the iron curtain fell, and Christianity blossomed forth like desert flowers after a rare spring rain. The dictators could not stop the church. In Ethiopia, in Latin America, ruthless puppets of Satan have tried to obliterate the church, but when they are gone, the church emerges stronger and more vibrant than ever. Christ is building His church on earth, and the gates of hell shall never prevail against it.

Jesus Is Inhabiting His Church

Not only is He building His church, but He is on earth spiritually, inhabiting His church. When a person believes in and receives Christ as his Lord and Savior, he is born again by the Holy Spirit. The eternal life which the new Christian is given at that point, however, is the life of Christ. In John 14:6 Jesus says, "I am the way, and the truth, and the life." In Colossians 3:4 we read, "When Christ who is our life appears, then you also will appear with Him in glory." The eternal life which we possess involves Jesus living in us.

That Jesus lives within each Christian gives us the hope of glory (Colossians 1:27). Because Jesus lives eternally and within us, we will live eternally, in glory. That is our hope. Because Jesus lives within us, we will be like Him (1 John 3:2). We will ultimately be able to escape this body and be given a new one (Romans 8:20–23). If you are satisfied with the body you have, wait twenty-five years. You will begin longing for a new one. Jesus' living within us enables us to live victoriously here on earth and with hope of eternal life in heaven with Him.

Like King Edward VI in *The Prince and the Pauper*, Christ is now on His throne, establishing His authority in heaven and earth. We feel frustrated that His "desired" will is not fulfilled as completely on earth as it is in heaven. We don't know God's timing for ending this great spiritual battle on earth and ushering in eternity. It could be today, it could be many years from now. We don't know why He does not limit the impact of sin more completely. When children learn that Satan is the original cause of sin on earth, that he is the king of this world and the prince of the power of the air, and that he is actively trying to deceive and destroy mankind, they frequently ask why God doesn't kill Satan. Theological splinters need to be sanded off that question, but at its core, it is quite valid.

Scripture answers it. At some future but already determined time, God will separate Satan from the redeemed world forever, and we will never have to suffer his presence or influence again. Until then, we must patiently wait for the hope of God to be fulfilled. And it will. Either we will die and go to heaven, or Christ will return before we die, thus ending Satan's influence. Until then, as the apostle John prayed in Revelation 22:20, "Come, Lord Jesus!"

Speed Bump!

Slow down to be sure you've gotten the main points of this chapter.

Question
Answer

Q1. Where is Jesus now?

A1. Jesus is in *heaven* now, sitting at the right hand of God the Father.

Q2. What is Jesus doing now in heaven?

A2. Jesus is *praying* to the Father on behalf of His children, and is *preparing* heaven for our arrival.

Q3. What is Jesus doing now on earth?

A3. Jesus is *building* His church.

Fill in the Blank

Question
Answer

Q1. Where is Jesus now?

A1. Jesus is in _____ now, sitting at the right hand of God the Father.

Q2. What is Jesus doing now in heaven?

A2. Jesus is _____ to the Father on behalf of His children, and is _____ heaven for our arrival.

Q3. What is Jesus doing now on earth?

A3. Jesus is _____ His church.

For Further Thought and Discussion

1. What do you think your reaction would be if you saw Jesus rise slowly from the earth and disappear into a cloud? What emotions would you be feeling? What thoughts would be running through your head?

2. Why do you think Jesus sits at the throne of the Father praying for us? Why isn't His accomplished work on the cross enough? Why does He have to pray for us on an ongoing basis also?

3. What preparations do you think Jesus has to make for us? If He created the universe in six days, do you think He is still preparing things for us, or is the work done by now, since He has been in heaven almost two thousand years?

4. Does it seem that Jesus has been successful or unsuccessful in building the church He promised to build?

5. In 1 Timothy 2:2, Paul admonishes us to pray for those who are in authority, "that we may lead a quiet and peaceable life in all godliness and reverence." This seems to have some influence on people being saved and coming "to the knowledge of the truth" (verse 4). How do you reconcile that with the fact that churches tend to decline after they have had long periods of "ease," while churches often strengthen and increase as a result of persecution?

What If I Don't Believe?

If I don't believe what Jesus is doing now, I not only run counter to the teachings of the Bible, but I also miss the encouragement of knowing that Jesus is concerned about me on an ongoing basis. I lose the joy of knowing that He is praying for me, that He is defending me before the courts of heaven when I sin, and that He is preparing a place for me for when I die or He returns. I also lose the confidence of believing that, in spite of how things look on the surface, Jesus is building His church, and the gates of hell are, in fact, not prevailing against it.

Further Study

1. Scripture

Several key passages in the Bible speak of what Jesus is doing now. They include:

- Hebrews 7:25

- Ephesians 1:18–23

- John 14:1–3

- Matthew 16:18

If you wish further study, read these passages and consider how they contribute to your understanding of what Jesus did and why.

2. Books

Several other books are very helpful in studying further this subject. They are listed below in general order of difficulty. If I could read only one of these, I would read the first one.

Know What You Believe, Paul Little
A Survey of Bible Doctrine, Charles Ryrie
Jesus Christ Our Lord, John Walvoord
The Words and Works of Jesus Christ, J. Dwight Pentecost

Joy is the serious business of heaven.
■ **C. S. Lewis**

12

What Will Jesus Do In Eternity?

Every human heart longs for eternity. The Bible tells us that God put that yearning there, but we would know it without the Bible. We see it in all ages, cultures, and peoples. We see it in burial practices. Egyptians mummified the bodies of their important leaders, hoping to preserve them for eternity. Some American Indians placed the bodies of their dead high in trees or other lofty places to make it easier for them to pass on to the spirit world. Vikings were reputed to send a dead body to sea in a boat set aflame. Boat and body burned and sank to the bottom of the ocean. This helped transport the spirit to the world beyond.

We see this longing for immortality in the common stories of the world. Even in our own fairy tales, the yearning comes through strongly, emerging symbolically from stories such as "Sleeping Beauty." She falls under the curse of a wicked person and goes into a death-like sleep. She can only be awakened by the kiss of a prince. He kisses her, raising her back to life, and they live happily ever after. It is interesting to me how closely a story such as that corresponds to the human condition. Sleeping Beauty is mankind. The curse is sin. The wicked person is Satan. The prince is Jesus. The reawakening is the new birth, and living happily ever after is heaven.

Other fairy tales have similar themes. In Snow White and the Seven Dwarfs, Snow White falls under a curse, and goes into a deep trance, and is reawakened by a prince, to live happily ever after. Cinderella is born to a happy and prosperous family, but both her mother and father die, and she falls into the hands of a wicked stepmother. Her life is cursed until she goes to a royal ball with the help of her fairy god-mother. There she meets a handsome prince and they fall in love. The handsome prince marries Cinderella and takes her away from the misery and pain of life with her wicked stepmother to live with him in the royal palace.

An entire volume could be written showing that eternity is placed in the heart of mankind. But these are simple and easily grasped examples. With the assumption that it will be good to us, we hunger for the future. Every December, the supermarket trash newspapers fill with predictions by psychics. (James Kennedy of Coral Ridge Ministries once followed the predictions of one psychic one year and learned that none of the predictions came true, unless they were so general that anyone could have made them.) These papers sell rapidly.

In this chapter, we learn that:

1. While we know little about the specifics, heaven will be a place of *holiness*, beauty and joy.
2. Jesus will judge humanity, marry His bride, and reign over *heaven*.
3. We will glorify God and *enjoy* Him forever.

The future is veiled, and for good reason. There have been times in my life that had I known what was going to happen, I would have been a basket-case waiting for the axe to fall. Still, the future draws us. We are eternal beings, created for a world other than this—destined for a better world than this. It is natural for us to look forward to it. Yet the Bible does not give us a lot of details about heaven and the future. Vance Havner, a witty preacher of an earlier generation, said if God had given us a clear picture of heaven, it would be like putting a plate of spinach in front of a young boy, with a chocolate cake at the other end of the table. It would be even harder for the young boy to get his spinach down, looking at the chocolate cake all the time.

The question, "What will Jesus do in eternity?" is of deep interest to us, not only because of our interest in God, but also because it affects what we will do in eternity. And while the Bible does not give us a lot of information about eternity, it does give us some, and that "some" can be very enlightening and encouraging.

What Will Heaven Be Like?

While we know little about the specifics, heaven will be a place of holiness, beauty, and joy.

We know very little about what heaven will be like, partly because the Bible is not very systematic or thorough in telling us and partly because we are not always sure whether the information in the Bible should be taken literally or figuratively. The Bible uses the word "heaven" 434 times. Sometimes, it means the starry heavens, other times it means the atmosphere around the earth, and other times the place where God dwells. We, of course, are interested in the place where God dwells, for where God dwells, there shall we dwell. The throne room of God is located there (Revelation 4:1–2).

Do you have trouble reading novels which have a lot of physical description in them? I do. I weary quickly, because, while I am sure the scene is very vivid in the writer's eye as he tries to describe it in such a way as to enable me to envision the same thing he is looking at, I'm afraid, for whatever reason, it never works very well with me. I read, "The sunlight filtered down through the trees until it disappeared like a soft blanket of dark green as the mist rose from the wet ground like an old friend to meet it. Small pink flowers lined a brook which wound its way through the lowland, stopping occasionally to play leapfrog with a large stone." Nothing much comes to mind. I'm pretty dull. Now, if you say, "It was a dark and stormy night," then all kinds of vivid pictures fill my mind. When it comes to literary descriptions, I'm pretty simple-minded.

In spite of that, the apostle John described a scene in heaven that even I can get some mental picture of:

> [I saw] a door standing open in heaven . . . and behold, a throne was standing in heaven, and One sitting on the throne. And He who was sitting was like a jasper stone and a sardius in appearance; and there was a rainbow around the throne, like an emerald in appearance. . . . And from the throne proceed flashes of lightning and sounds and peals of thunder . . . and before the throne there was, as it were, a sea of glass like crystal." (from Revelation 4:1–6 NASB).

I can't visualize some of the description, because I don't know what a jasper stone or sardius look like. But the rest of it I can picture. It must be an amazing place. Certainly, there is no place like it on earth, this place where God dwells. It is like comparing a gully to the Grand Canyon, but if you have ever seen the *Wizard of Oz*, the "throne room" where Oz is has a floor like glass, vast high ceilings, flashes of lightening and peals of thunder, and great billows of smoke. Most impressive! It is wonderful and terrifying at the same time. I have often wondered if the producers of the movie read the book of Revelation before coming up with their throne room set for that movie.

Why I need to know this:

1. If I believe that heaven in a place of holiness, beauty, and joy, I realize it is a place superior to earth. The beauty of heaven will far surpass the beauty of earth. In addition, there will be none of the ugliness, none of the pain, none of the sorrow. It will help me be willing to live more for the things of heaven and less for the things of earth.

2. If I understand that Jesus will judge humanity, I will live carefully on earth. I will strive to live a good life, and avoid known sin. I will look forward to the joy of reigning with Christ, and of being His bride.

3. If I believe that my purpose in being created is to glorify God and enjoy Him forever, it will cause my heart to turn toward Him more fully, to get to know Him better, to try to serve Him more faithfully, and to look forward to the day when I will live with Him in heaven.

In addition to this heaven, of which we are told little, the Bible talks about a "New Jerusalem" coming down out of heaven as a bride adorned for her bridegroom. I was taught, both in church and later in seminary, that the New Jerusalem was a literal place, as the Bible says, 1500 miles wide, 1500 miles long, and 1500 miles high, streets of gold, gates of pearl, and so on. This New Jerusalem seems to be suspended above an oceanless new earth (Revelation 21:1–27). Well, several questions arise. Who lives in the New Jerusalem? Who lives on the new earth? Does anyone live in the new heaven, beyond the New Jerusalem? Conceivably, the new heaven is vast, yet the New Jerusalem is comparatively small. Many Bible teachers believe they know the answer to these questions. Unfortunately for the average lay person, the Bible teachers don't all agree. That is what heaven looks like, incomplete as the description is.

But what will we be like when we get there? Well, the Bible says, "Beloved, now we are children of God, and it has not appeared as yet what we shall be. We know that, when He appears, we shall be like Him, because we shall see Him just as He is" (1 John 3:2 NASB). We shall be like Him spiritually in that we will no longer sin, and we will think and do only righteous things. Sarcasm will no longer drip from our tongues. Anger will no longer vent through our mouths. Lust will no longer grip our hearts. Envy, hatred, lack of forgiveness, fear, anxiety, materialism, selfishness—all will vanish like darkness on a bright and early dawn.

We shall be like Him physically. Jesus' resurrection body is glorified. That is, you can tell that it is Jesus, but the heavenly body has characteristics that transcend those of a natural body. Obviously, that body will not age or die. But beyond that, His body is dazzling light. Matthew wrote "And . . .

Heaven will be better than anything we experience on earth

Jesus took with Him Peter and James and John his brother, and brought them up to a high mountain by themselves. And He was transfigured before them; and His face shone like the sun, and His garments became as white as light" (Matthew 17:1–2 NASB). Can you imagine? The natural eye would not even be able to look for long at His face. The apostle John wrote of his vision of Jesus in the book of Revelation,

> I saw . . . one like a son of man, clothed in a robe reaching to the feet, and girded across His breast with a golden girdle. And His head and His hair were white like white wool, like snow; and His eyes were like a flame of fire; and His feet were like burnished bronze, when it has been caused to glow in a furnace, and His voice was like the sound of many waters. . . . and His face was like the sun shining in its strength (1:12–16 NASB).

Amazing! Then John wrote, "And when I saw Him, I fell at His feet as dead" (verse 17). Well, I don't wonder! Who wouldn't? And yet, from all indications, that is generally what we will look like when we get to heaven. And, if we are to be like Jesus, we will be able to walk through walls (if there are any in heaven), appear and disappear, travel at the speed of thought, and so on. Lumbago? Never. Rheumatism? Not in any joint! Lower back pain? No chance. As I said earlier, if this doesn't make you long for heaven, give yourself twenty years.

What Will Jesus Do in Eternity?

Jesus will judge humanity, marry His bride, and reign over heaven.

Jesus Will Judge Humanity

Jesus will do several things to begin eternity, final things from the temporal world that need to be finished. Again, theologians and Bible teachers do not all agree on what these things are and when they will happen. They do not agree on how much of it is to be interpreted literally and how much symbolically. But we can generalize and say some things that most everyone will agree with. First, at some point, Jesus will assess the lives of all people. He will reward His spiritual children for their good works on earth, and He will judge those who rejected Him.

Concerning the rewards for His children, we see three scenes in the New Testament. The first pictures a courtroom. "For we shall all stand before the judgment seat of God. For it is written, 'As I live, says the Lord, every knee shall bow to Me, and every tongue shall give praise to God.' So then each one of us shall give account of himself to God" (Romans 14:10–12 NASB). In this, we learn the inescapable fact that one day everyone will stand before God to give an account of himself.

The second scene describes a building.

For no man can lay a foundation other than the one which is laid, which is Jesus Christ. Now if any man builds upon the foundation with gold, silver, precious stones, wood, hay, straw, each man's work will become evident; for the day will show it, because it is to be revealed with fire; and the fire itself will test the quality of each man's work. If any man's work which he has built upon it remains, he shall receive a reward. If any man's work is burned up, he shall suffer loss; but he himself shall be saved, yet so as through fire (1 Corinthians 3:11–15 NASB).

Here we learn that our bad works will be destroyed, but our good works will be rewarded. Even though we have some bad works, they will not destroy us. Our good works will be beautiful and precious.

The third scene portrays an athletic contest.

Do you not know that those who run in a race all run, but only one receives the prize? Run in such a way that you may win. And everyone who competes in the games exercises self-control in all things. They then do it to receive a perishable wreath, but we an imperishable. Therefore I run in such a way, as not without aim; I box in such a way, as not beating the air; but I buffet my body and make it my slave, lest possibly, after I have preached to others, I myself should be disqualified" (1 Corinthians 9:24–27 NASB).

In this picture, we learn that we can lose the imperishable prize we strive for by being undisciplined or by not competing according to the rules.

Regardless of when these events happen, we cannot miss the

fact that Jesus will review each life. That must come early on in the eternal state, or else we would not know what our eternal state will be.

Concerning those who have rejected Him, we read in Revelation 20:11–15:

And I saw a great white throne and Him who sat upon it, from whose presence earth and heaven fled away, and no place was found for them. And I saw the dead, the great and the small, standing before the throne, and books were opened; and another book was opened, which is the book of life; and the dead were judged from the things which were written in the books, according to their deeds. And the sea gave up the dead which were in it, and death and Hades gave up the dead which were in them; and they were judged, every one of them according to their deeds. And death and Hades were thrown into the lake of fire. This is the second death, the lake of fire. And if anyone's name was not found written in the book of life, he was thrown into the lake of fire. (NASB)

This is a terrifying scene, and one we wish were not inevitable. Nevertheless, there it is, a sober warning to those who would reject Jesus. Let theologians and scholars debate all they will over what is literal and what is figurative, but if you do not like going to a dentist to get a root canal done, you want nothing to do with hell. If you do not enjoy absolute solitude (solitary confinement is considered the worst form of punishment in prison), you want nothing to do with hell.

Jesus Will Marry His Bride

A second thing He will do is marry His bride, the church, and have a great feast:

And a voice came from the throne, saying, "Give praise to our God, all you His bond-servants, you who fear Him, the small and the great." And I heard, as it were, the voice of a great multitude and as the sound of many waters and as the sound of mighty peals of thunder, saying, "Hallelujah! For the Lord our God, the Almighty, reigns. Let us rejoice and be glad and give the glory to Him, for the marriage of the Lamb has come and His bride has made herself ready." And it was given to her to clothe herself in fine linen, bright and clean; for the fine linen is the righteous acts of the saints. And he said to me, "Write, 'Blessed are those who are invited to the marriage supper of the Lamb.'" And he said to me, "These are true words of God" (Revelation 19:5–9 NASB).

Again, Bible teachers disagree on exactly what this means, how much is literal and how much is symbolic. But on this we can all agree: The church, the totality of all believers in Jesus, is elevated to a wonderful place and linked to Jesus in a special relationship for all eternity. In the Old Testament, Israel is referred to as the bride of God. In the New Testament, the church is referred to as the bride of Christ. There seems to be a special relationship between God the Father and Israel, and between Jesus and the church. This ought not be pressed too far, however, because while God is three, He is also one. Nevertheless, to repeat, one of the earliest things that Jesus does in eternity is to marry His bride, the church.

Jesus Will Reign over Heaven

A third thing which Jesus will do in eternity is to reign over heaven.

And the seventh angel sounded; and there arose loud voices in heaven, saying, "The kingdom of the world has become the kingdom of our Lord, and of His Christ; and He will reign forever and ever." And the twenty-four elders, who sit on their thrones before God, fell on their faces and worshipped God, "We give Thee thanks, O Lord God, the Almighty, who art and who wast, because Thou hast taken Thy great power and hast begun to reign" (Revelation 11:15–17 NASB).

What this means, we don't really know. Who will He reign over? Well, there are all the believers in God in the Old Testament and Jesus in the New Testament. There are all the angels who number in the "ten thousands times ten thousands," which is probably a metaphor for a virtually numberless host. And there will be the new heavens, the new earth, and the New Jerusalem.

What Will We Do In Eternity?
We will glorify God and enjoy Him forever.

It is impossible to discuss what Jesus will do in eternity without touching on what we will do in eternity, because Jesus' activities and ours are woven together forever. We, as Christians, are part of the church, and therefore, part of the bride of Christ. We will be wed to Him for eternity. What does this mean? Well, beyond what we have already said, there are few clues. As the Westminster Confession, a well-known document from church history says, we shall "glorify God and enjoy Him forever." While that is gloriously true, we will be active in other ways.

We Shall Govern

We shall reign with Christ forever.

> For this reason I endure all things for the sake of those who are chosen, that they also may obtain the salvation which is in Christ Jesus and with it eternal glory. It is a trustworthy statement: For if we died with Him, we shall also live with Him; If we endure, we shall also reign with Him (2 Timothy 2:10–12 NASB).

Reign over whom? Over each other? Over angels? Over beings that do not yet exist, or that we do not know about? We don't know.

The "spirits of just men made perfect" (Hebrews 12:23) will be in the "city of the living God, the heavenly Jerusalem" (verse 22), and we will assist in governing the whole. Perhaps this is tied in with the parable in Luke 19 in which a servant who was faithful in little on earth is, in heaven, given authority over cities. In Matthew, the servant who had been given five talents and had gained five more was promised the privilege of ruling over many things (25:20–21).

We Will Worship

In the fourth chapter of the Gospel of John, we read, "But an hour is coming, and now is, when the true worshipers shall worship the Father in spirit and truth; for such people the Father seeks to be His worshipers. God is spirit, and those who worship Him must worship in spirit and truth" (verses 23–24 NASB). One of God's primary purposes is to gather to Himself those who would worship Him. Worship will be, perhaps, the central activity in heaven. Whenever we glimpse God in celestial glory we see worship going on (Isaiah 6:1–8; Revelation 4—5; 19:1–8). In fact, in Revelation 19, we behold a scene in heaven which focuses on worship:

After these things I heard, as it were, a loud voice of a great multitude in heaven, saying, "Hallelujah! Salvation and glory and power belong to our God; because His judgments are true and righteous." . . . And a second time they said, "Hallelujah!" And the twenty-four elders and the four living creatures fell down and worshipped God who sits on the throne saying, "Amen. Hallelujah!" And a voice came from the throne, saying, "Give praise to our God, all you His bond-servants, you who fear Him, the small and the great." And I heard, as it were, the voice of a great multitude and as the sound of many waters and as the sound of mighty peals of thunder, saying, "Hallelujah! For the Lord our God, the Almighty, reigns. Let us rejoice and be glad and give the glory to Him, for the marriage of the Lamb has come and His bride has made herself ready." And it was given to her to clothe herself in fine linen, bright and clean; for the fine linen is the righteous acts of the saints (Revelation 19:1–8 NASB).

Music will play an important part. In Revelation 4 and 5, we peek into the throne room of heaven. The Father and Son are surrounded by angels and saints, with a lot of singing going on:

After these things I looked, and behold, a door standing open in heaven . . . and behold, a throne was standing in heaven, and One sitting on the throne. And He who was sitting was like a jasper stone and a sardius in appearance; and there was a rainbow around the throne, like an emerald in appearance. And around the throne were twenty-four thrones; and upon the thrones I saw twenty-four elders sitting, clothed in white garments, and golden crowns on their heads. And from the throne proceed flashes of lightning and sounds and peals of thunder. And there were seven lamps of fire burning before the throne, which are the seven Spirits of God; and before the throne there was, as it were, a sea of glass like crystal . . . the twenty-four elders will fall down before Him who sits on the throne, and will worship Him who lives forever and ever, and will cast their crowns before the throne, saying, "Worthy art Thou, our Lord and our God, to receive glory and honor and power; for Thou didst create all things, and because of Thy will they existed, and were created.". . . The four living creatures and the twenty-four elders fell down before the Lamb, having each one a harp, and golden bowls full of incense, which are the prayers of the saints. And they sang a new song, saying, "Worthy art Thou to take the book, and to break its seals; for Thou wast slain, and didst purchase for God with Thy blood men from every tribe and tongue and people and nation. And Thou hast made them to be a kingdom and priests to our God; and they will reign upon the earth." And I looked, and I heard the voice of many angels around the throne and the living creatures and the elders; and the number of them was myriads of myriads, and thousands of thousands, saying with a loud voice, "Worthy is the Lamb that was slain to receive power and riches and wisdom and might and honor and glory and blessing." And every created thing which is in heaven and on the earth and under the earth and on the sea, and all things in them, I heard saying, "To Him who sits on the throne, and to the Lamb, be blessing and honor and glory and dominion forever and ever." And the four living creatures kept saying, "Amen." And the elders fell down and worshipped (Revelation 4:1–6, 10–11; 5:8–14 NASB).

What a scene! Worship will be the central activity in heaven, and we will love it. Eternity's finest choir will be singing the most glorious music with totally pure hearts, and we will watch our God as He receives our worship.

We Will Serve the Lord

Just as we serve Jesus here on earth, we will continue to serve Him in heaven. While we might not know what that service will include, a number of things we will do in heaven will be a continuation of our "bond-servant" relationship to Jesus here on earth. This service will be, however,

> work as free from care and toil and fatigue as is the wing-stroke of the jubilant lark when it soars into the sunlight of a fresh, clear day and spontaneously and for self-relief, pours out its thrilling carol. Work up there is a matter of self-relief, as well as a matter of obedience to the ruling will of God. It is work according to one's tastes and delight and ability. If tastes vary there, if abilities vary there, then occupations will vary there (David Gregg, *The Heaven-Life*, 62).

We Will Fellowship

If unity on earth is God's priority for us (John 17:21), it seems likely that unity will be a priority in heaven. Fellowship, the establishing of satisfying relationships, is one of the best things about earth. Someone once said that without a friend, the world is but a wilderness. How true. Ralph Waldo Emerson said, "A friend may well be reckoned a masterpiece of nature." Surely it will be a part of heaven. It has also been said that friendship improves happiness and eases misery by doubling our joy and dividing our grief. Since there will be no grief in heaven, there will only be the doubling and tripling of our joy.

How I love a good conversation! It thrills me when someone engages me in discussion of intense mutual interest, and off we go into conversation and fellowship. What pleasure! Can you imagine conversing not only with the famous Christians of this world, but also with the nameless Christians (as you and I will be) whose stories will be just as interesting and just as meaningful as anyone else's? Our greatest joy will be getting to know God, but if heaven is anything like earth in regard to fellowship, we will also enjoy getting to know others who love and serve God.

What else might we do in heaven? It is hard to know. It will be more enjoyable, more fulfilling, more thrilling than living here on earth. For many people, especially those whose lives have a lot of pain, this world is not an enjoyable place. Many Christians living in comparatively easy circumstances might not long for heaven. But I assure you, the Christian in Ethiopia who cannot feed his family, whose children are diseased, who fears revolutionary soldiers killing his family for their faith—he is looking forward to heaven. And in heaven, I think we might sit at his feet. Giants walk the earth of whom the world knows nothing.

The best of earth only hints of the glories of heaven.

So it appears that there will be plenty to do, and many opportunities to worship and sing praises to our God. If earth is any indication of the image of God, it will not be a place where we sit around on clouds and strum harps. Rather, it will be a dynamic place of relationship, creativity, beauty, and worship. I saw a bumper sticker once that said, "The worst day fishing is better than the best day working." Well, it seems reasonable to speculate that any day in heaven will be better than the best day on earth.

Conclusion

From the glory of heaven as God to a life of love, obedience, and humility as man, a life fully and mysteriously human and divine, to death as a capital criminal on a Roman cross—this is the story of Jesus, our savior; Jesus, the one who offers Himself fully as the sacrifice that gives us life.

Children have such a difficult time grasping what their parents sacrifice for them. In fact, it usually isn't until they perform similar sacrifices for their own children that they begin to grasp how much their parents loved them. The time, emotional energy, money, physical strength, personal desires, all sacrificed for the sake of the child, are often taken for granted, as though it is all owed to him. He may not be mature enough to take it any other way.

We face a similar danger as Christians, not being able to grasp all that Jesus has done for us. We risk taking it all for granted, thinking that what Jesus has done for us is owed us, or that it was of little consequence. Ted Engstrom, in his book *The Fine Art of Friendship*, tells a story which helps us grasp some of what Jesus has done for us. A young husband with a crippling, terminal neurological disease writes a letter to the unborn child in his wife's womb which he may never live to see:

> Your mother is very special. Few men know what it is like to receive appreciation for taking their wives out to dinner when it entails what it does for us. It means that she has to dress me, shave me, brush my teeth, comb my hair; wheel me out of the house and down the steps, open the garage and put me in the car, take the pedals off the chair, stand me up, sit me in the seat of the car, twist me around so that I'm comfortable, fold the wheelchair, put it in the car, go around to the other side of the car, start it up, back it out, get out of the car, pull the garage door down, get back into the car, and drive off to the restaurant. And then, it starts all over again: she gets out of the car, unfolds the wheelchair, opens the door, spins me around, stands me up, seats me in the wheelchair, pushes the pedals out, closes and locks the car, wheels me into the restaurant, then takes the pedals off the wheelchair so I won't be uncomfortable. We sit down to have dinner, and she feeds me throughout the entire meal. And when it's over she pays the bill, pushes the wheelchair out to the car again, and reverses the same routine. And when it's over—finished—with real warmth she'll say, "Honey, thank you for taking me out to dinner." I never quite know what to answer (103–104).

When I read this story, I felt I ought to take off my shoes . . . that I was standing on holy ground. That woman is a saint. She has the thumbprint of God deep in her soul. Even so, without in any way diminishing what she did, it pales in comparison to what Jesus has done for us. If we truly grasped what Jesus has done for us, we wouldn't know quite what to answer. He gave up the glories of heaven, endured the indignities of life on earth, let those whom He could have annihilated drive nails through his hands and feet and hang him on a cross, and He let His Father place the sin of the world on Him.

And when that was done, he said, "Please accept my offer to forgive your sins, to give you eternal live, to put my Spirit within you, and to give you a new heart. Please come to live with me for eternity, so that I can show my limitless, unending love to you. Please live with me in perfect fellowship and harmony in paradise forever."

The more we understand of Jesus' sacrifice, and of His outpouring of love, the less we know quite how to answer.

What do we say? It is feeble, but say it with me:

"Lord Jesus, I don't know quite what to say. Your love conquers me. It overwhelms me. I surrender to your love. As best I can, still walking in this corrupted and rebellious body of sin, I give myself to you. Instruct me, and I will learn. Command me and I will obey. Lead me and I will follow. I kneel before you now, my Lord and my God, and say forever, 'Thy will be done.' Amen."

Speed Bump!

Slow down to be sure you've gotten the main points of this chapter.

*Q***uestion**
*A***nswer**

Q1. What will heaven be like?

A1. While we know little about the specifics, heaven will be a place of *holiness*, beauty and joy.

Q2. What will Jesus do in eternity?

A2. Jesus will judge humanity, marry His bride, and reign over *heaven*.

Q3. What will we do in eternity?

A3. We will glorify God and *enjoy* Him forever.

Fill In the Blank

Question
Answer

Q1. What will heaven be like?

A1. While we know little about the specifics, heaven will be a place of _____, beauty and joy.

Q2. What will Jesus do in eternity?

A2. Jesus will judge humanity, marry His bride, and reign over _____.

Q3. What will we do in eternity?

A3. We will glorify God and _____ Him forever.

For Further Thought and Discussion

1. We don't hear much about judgment and hell these days. The concept has become socially unacceptable. Yet the judgment of God over men is an inescapable component of Scriptural teaching. Why do you think you hear little about it?

2. What do you think about it? Do you enjoy hearing about it? If you knew that a preacher were going to preach on the subject the next Sunday, would you be eager to go? Why or why not?

3. Jesus' marrying His bride is a word picture, meaning He will enter into a special relationship with all Christians. Think about the strong marriages you know of on earth, and by analyzing them, what speculations do you think might be valid to make about our relationship with Christ in heaven?

4. Have you ever given much thought to the idea that you will enjoy God forever? What do you think there will be to enjoy? Remember that at age 1, one of your greatest joys was to pick things up off the floor and put them into your mouth. At age 6, you loved to play simple games and imaginary games. At age 16, your greatest interest might have been to drive a car, and so on, into adulthood. The point is, our interests change. It is reasonable to assume, then, that we will be extremely interested in things in heaven that are not powerfully interesting or enjoyable now. What do you think some of those things might be?

What If I Don't Believe

1. If I don't believe what the Bible teaches about eternity, I have little or nothing to look forward to when I die. Considering that everyone dies, it is a gloomy thing not to have something to look forward to after death. Even more than gloomy, it is terrifying if we believe that there is life after death, and that we might be separated from God forever.

2. If I don't believe that God judges people after death, I may be deceived into rejecting Him in this life, only to have Him reject me in the next.

3. If I don't believe that I will enjoy heaven, I will have little reason to want to go there.

For Further Study

1. Scripture
Several key passages in the Bible speak of what Jesus will do in eternity. They include:

- John 14:1–3

- Revelation 4 and 5

- 1 Corinthians 15

- Revelation 1:10–18

- Revelation 19:1–9

- Revelation 21 and 22

If you wish further study, read these passages and consider how they contribute to your understanding of what Jesus did and why.

2. Books
Several other books are very helpful in studying further this subject. They are listed below in general order of difficulty. If I could only read one of these, I would read the first one.

Know What You Believe, Paul Little
Heaven, W.A. Criswell and Paige Patterson
Heaven, the Heart's Greatest Longing, Peter Kreeft
The Words and Works of Jesus Christ, J. Dwight Pentecost

Bibliography

Blaiklock, E.M. *Jesus Christ, Man or Myth*. Nashville: Thomas Nelson Publishers, 1984.

Canfield, Jack and Hansen, Mark. *Chicken Soup for the Soul*. Deerfield Beach, FL: Health Communications, Inc., 1993.

Elwell, Walter A. *The Evangelical Dictionary of Theology*. Grand Rapids: Baker Book House, 1984.

Engstrom, Ted. *The Fine Art of Friendship*. Nashville: Thomas Nelson Publishers, 1985.

Green, Michael. *Who Is This Jesus?* Nashville: Thomas Nelson Publishers, 1992.

Kennedy, James. *What if Jesus Had Never Been Born?* Nashville: Thomas Nelson Publishers, 1993.

Kenyon, Sir Frederick. *The Bible and Archaeology*. New York: Harper & Row, 1940.

Lewis, C.S. *Mere Christianity*. New York: The MacMillian Company, 1943.

Lewis, C.S. *Surprised by Joy*. New York: Harcourt, Brace and World, 1955.

Little, Paul. *Know Why You Believe*. Downer's Grove, IL: InterVarsity Press, 1988.

McDowell, Josh. *Evidence that Demands a Verdict*. San Bernardino, CA: Here's Life Publishers, 1972, 1979.

Montgomery, John Warwick. *History and Christianity*. Downer's Grove, IL: InterVarsity Press, 1971.

Sherwin-White, A.N. *Roman Society and Roman Law in the New Testament*. Twin Brooks Reprint Series. Grand Rapids: Baker Book House, 1992.

Vallery-Radot, Rene. *The Life of Pasteur*. Trans. R.L. Devonshire. Garden City, NJ: Doubleday, Page and Company, 1923.

Master Review

Question
Answer

Chapter 1

Q1. What do you mean when you say "Jesus"?

A1. Jesus of Nazareth is the *divine* Son of God, the second member of the Trinity, and the Savior of humankind.

Q2. Why believe Jesus was God?

A2. We believe Jesus was God because the *Scriptures* declare Him to be God, and His words and works prove Him to be God.

Q3. Why believe Jesus was a man?

A3. We believe Jesus was a man because the *Scriptures* declare Him to be a man, and His words and works prove Him to be a man.

Chapter 2

Q1. What was Jesus like, being both God and man?

A1. Jesus possessed all the attributes of a man, while never *giving up* any attributes of God.

Q2. Why was Jesus subject to God the Father?

A2. Jesus was subject to the Father because, while all members of the Godhead are equal, they have distinct *roles* in their saving activity toward humanity. God the Father has always been in loving authority, and Jesus has always been in loving submission.

Q3. How did Jesus influence others?

A3. Jesus' *powerful* presence moved people either to accept or reject Him.

Chapter 3

Q1. What did Jesus teach about humankind's greatest need?

A1. Jesus taught that humankind is spiritually *lost* and needed to be saved.

Q2. What did Jesus teach about true righteousness?

A2. Jesus taught that true righteousness is *internal*, not external.

Q3. What did Jesus teach is the most important commandment?

A3. Jesus taught that we should *love* God with all our heart and soul and mind.

Chapter 4

Q1. Why did Jesus perform miracles?

A1. To validate the new *message* of salvation He was bringing to humanity.

Q2. Why did Jesus confront the religious establishment?

A2. To reveal the *barrenness* of their spirituality and to open access to God for the multitudes.

Q3. How did Jesus prepare for His departure?

A3. By equipping a core of *disciples* to carry on His work in His absence.

Chapter 5

Q1. What did Jesus reveal to us about God's love for us?

A1. Jesus revealed that God's love is so great that *nothing* can keep us from God if we will but come to Him.

Q2. What did Jesus reveal about how to live?

A2. Jesus revealed that life is to be lived in total *trust* in, and *obedience* to, our heavenly Father.

Q3. What did Jesus' life accomplish for our eternal destiny?

A3. Jesus made it possible for us to be *forgiven* of our sins, reconciled to God, and made ready for heaven.

Chapter 6

Q1. How can we meet Jesus?

A1. By *believing* in Him, accepting Him as our Savior, repenting of our old life and giving our lives over to Him.

Q2. How can we grow in our knowledge of Jesus through the Scriptures?

A2. We can grow in our knowledge of Christ by learning well the *Scriptures*, with a compliant heart.

Q3. How can we grow in our knowledge of Jesus through experience?

A2. We get to know Jesus better by *imitating* His example of living, emulating other good Christians, and observing our own spiritual experience.

Chapter 7

Q1. How do we make our decision about who Jesus is?

A1. We make our decision about who Jesus is either by letting the *evidence* speak for itself to our open mind, or by deciding ahead of time that the evidence cannot be believed.

Q2. What does the evidence suggest about the life of Jesus?

A2. More evidence supports the historical *existence* of Jesus than any other figure of antiquity.

Q3. What secular evidence do we have of Jesus' existence?

A3. Evidence from secular writers contemporary with Jesus is scant, but several key and *convincing* sources exist.

Q4. What archeological evidence do we have of Jesus' life?

A4. Very early archeological evidence, like early historical references, is not overabundant, but is highly *credible.*

Chapter 8

Q1. What impact has Jesus had on social issues?

A1. Jesus has *improved* the quality of education, health care, and poverty relief all over the world.

Q2. What impact has Jesus had on government?

A2. Jesus had encouraged the *protection* of the individual wherever government has respected biblical principles.

Q3. What has the twentieth century taught us?

A3. The twentieth century has taught us that when a nation forgets God, *calamity* results.

Chapter 9

Q1. Did Jesus fulfill prophecy?

A1. Against all odds, Jesus *fulfilled* all prophecies necessary to qualify as the Messiah.

Q2. Are Jesus's words the words of God?

A2. Jesus' *statements* and claims exceeded the credibility of a human being, and could only be the words of God.

Q3. Are Jesus' acts the acts of God?

A3. Jesus' *deeds* surpassed human ability, and could only be the works of God.

Chapter 10

Q1. Did Jesus die?

A1. The declaration of Scripture, the description of the crucifixion, and the testimony of history all agree that Jesus *died*.

Q2. Was the tomb empty?

A2. The declaration of Scripture, the description of post-crucifixion events, and the testimony of history all agree that Jesus' tomb was *empty*.

Q3. How can the empty tomb be explained?

A3. The empty tomb can be explained with any credibility only by saying that Jesus *rose* from the dead.

Q4. Did the resurrection happen?

A4. The case for the resurrection is *overwhelming* if you accept evidence at face value, as you would for any other historical event.

Chapter 11

Q1. Where is Jesus now?

A1. Jesus is in *heaven* now, sitting at the right hand of God the Father.

Q2. What is Jesus doing now in heaven?

A2. Jesus is *praying* to the Father on behalf of His children, and is *preparing* heaven for our arrival.

Q3. What is Jesus doing now on earth?

A3. Jesus is *building* His church.

Chapter 12

Q1. What will heaven be like?

A1. While we know little about the specifics, heaven will be a place of *holiness*, beauty and joy.

Q2. What will Jesus do in eternity?

A2. Jesus will judge humanity, marry His bride, and reign over *heaven*.

Q3. What will we do in eternity?

A3. We will glorify God and *enjoy* Him forever.

About the Author

Max Anders is a pastor at heart who applies the truths of God's word to people's everyday lives. An original team member with Walk Thru the Bible Ministries and pastor of a mega-church for a number of years before beginning his speaking and writing ministry, Max has traveled extensively, speaking to thousands across the country.

His books include *30 Days to Understanding the Bible, 30 Days to Understanding the Christian Life, 30 Days to Understanding What Christians Believe,* and (as co-author) *Drawing Near.* He holds a Master of Theology degree from Dallas Theological Seminary and a doctorate from Western Seminary in Portland, Oregon.

If you are interested in having Max Anders speak at your conference, church, or special event, please call interAct Speaker's Bureau at 1-800-370-9932.